SOCCER

CROWOOD SPORTS GUIDES

SOCCER

TECHNIQUE • TACTICS • TRAINING

Sean Callery

The Crowood Press

First published in 1991 by
The Crowood Presss Ltd
Ramsbury, Marlborough
Wiltshire SN8 2HR

This impression 1995

British Library Cataloguing in Publication Data

Callery, Sean
    Soccer: technique, tactics, training.
    1. Association football. Techniques
    I. Title
    796.3342

ISBN 1 85223 542 X

Acknowledgements

Many thanks to the first team players of Hook Norton Football Club (sponsored by
The Hook Norton Brewery Co. Ltd.) and their mananger Hubie Stowe for their help
with the photographs in this book. Grateful thanks also to photographer Gray
Mortimore at Allsport UK Ltd., and my wife Emma who puts up with my soccer
obsession.

Throughout this book the pronouns 'he', 'his' and 'him' have been used. This means no
disrespect to the growing number of women who enjoy the game, and all advice
applies equally to both sexes.

Typeset by Chippendale Type Ltd., Otley, West Yorkshire.
Printed and bound by Times Offset.

CONTENTS

PREFACE

Soccer is a simple game. It is also one of the most enjoyable and popular contact sports in the world, and many believe the most exciting to watch. This book is designed to help you enjoy the game, by advising players on improving their skills, fitness and tactical awareness. The game combines opportunities for individual expression with a strong element of team work. A soccer match is a series of improvized moves (with a few pre-planned set-pieces) in which individuals work together to achieve an objective. It is also great fun, excellent physical exercise and deeply satisfying. One of the beauties of the game is that it can be played almost anywhere: many great players learned their basic skills kicking a tennis ball or even a tin can around on the street or an open area. However sophisticated the game becomes at the higher level, with complex tactical plans and new formations, its basic format remains the same: eleven players kicking the ball around.

PART I
THE GAME

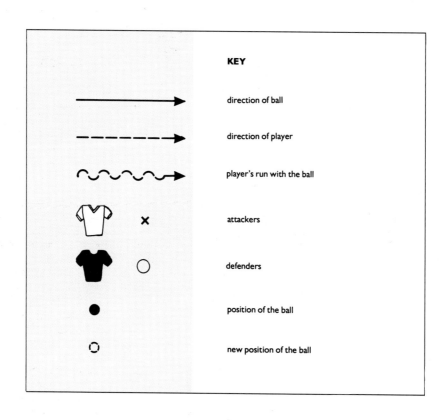

KEY

direction of ball

direction of player

player's run with the ball

attackers

defenders

position of the ball

new position of the ball

CHAPTER I

RULES

Soccer is a team game in which two sides of eleven players compete to direct the ball into the opposing team's goal. The remainder of this chapter gives a basic summary of the game, and throughout the book other relevant points of law are noted.

The Pitch

A soccer pitch is oblong and can be between 100yd (90m) and 130yd (120m) long, and 50yd (45m) to 100yd (90m) wide. In the centre of each short side is the goal which is 8yd (7.3m) wide and 8ft (2.44m) high. Around it are two boxes: one is 6yd (5.5m) deep and 20yd (18.3m) across (known as the six-yard box); the other is the penalty area, which is 18yd (16.5m) deep and 44yd (40.3m) across. The penalty area marks the zone in which the goalkeeper is allowed to handle the ball.

The penalty spot is 12yd (11m) from the centre of the goal. Part of a circle is formed on a radius 10yd (9.15m) from this spot in the space outside the penalty area. This is the 'semi-circle'. Half-way along the pitch is another line, the centre of which marks the centre spot, and around this is a circle at a radius of 10yd (9.15m).

This area is the field of play. If the ball leaves this area, it is deemed out of play until it can be returned through either a throw-in (from the side-line), a corner kick (from a 1yd (1m) quarter-circle in the corner of the pitch), or a goal kick (from the six-yard box). In each of these cases, possession goes to the team which did not touch the ball last.

The dimensions of a soccer pitch are illustrated in Fig 1 overleaf which also highlights the three thirds of the pitch as discussed in this book.

The Ball

This is round, with a circumference of 27–28in (68–71cm) and is made of an inflated leather or other approved material casing. The ball must weigh between 14–16oz (396–453g), and the pressure of the air in it should be equal to 0.6–1.1 atm (600–110 gr/cm^2). Younger players can use a smaller ball if they choose.

The Teams

There are eleven players in a team. Each team has a goalkeeper, who is the only player permitted to handle the ball, and is only to do this inside his own penalty area. Players can change positions at will, although if one is to change with the goalkeeper, the referee must be informed. A number of substitutes (usually two, but there are many variations) are allowed, each to replace one member of his own team provided the referee is notified.

The Officials

The match is controlled by the referee who stays on the pitch during the game, helped by two linesmen who patrol the side-lines and monitor whether the ball goes out of play on their side of the pitch. They also inform the referee of any

infringements to the rules. The referee can stop play at any time, and can discipline players for misdemeanours. The referee's decision is final and should not be challenged.

The Match

Matches are played for 45 minutes each way (sometimes less for youngsters) with a break of 10 minutes. The winner is the team which scores the most goals; a goal is scored when the whole of the ball crosses the goal-line between the goal-posts. If no goals or an equal number are scored, the match is drawn. In the case of some cup matches, a drawn match is continued through two extra periods of 15 minutes each way (called 'extra time'). If the score is still equal, a rematch is played, or the tie may be settled by penalties.

Team captains toss a coin to decide who will kick off for the game. At this point both teams must be in their own halves, with the opposing team at least 10yd (9m) from the ball (in other words, outside of the centre circle). Kick off is made from the centre spot and the ball must move forward, with the kicker forbidden to touch the ball again before another player has touched it. After a goal is scored, play resumes with a kick off by the team which suffered the goal. Play is continuous unless the referee stops it for an infringement or for another reason.

Free Kicks

These are awarded for infringements of the rules, and are taken from the location of the offence as indicated by the referee. Depending on the severity of the offence, free kicks can be direct (in other words, a shot can be struck directly into the

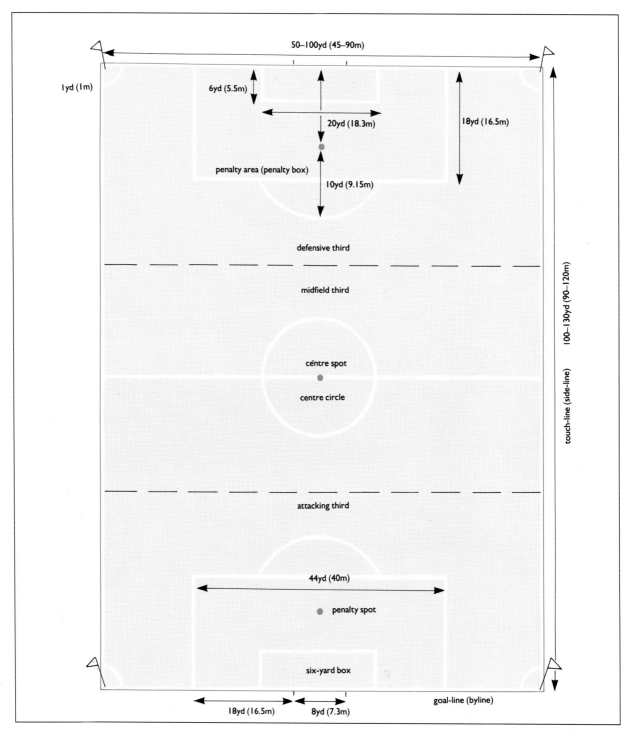

Fig 1 *Soccer pitch dimensions, with the three thirds of the pitch referred to in this book highlighted.*

opposing net); or indirect, meaning that a ball stuck straight into the goal would not count as a score. In the latter case, the referee holds his arm aloft until a second touch is made on the ball. Opposing players must stand at least 10yd (9m) from the ball until a free kick is struck.

If an offence is committed inside the penalty area, the referee can award a penalty. This is a direct free kick in which the ball is placed on the penalty spot and all players except the goalkeeper must leave the penalty area until the ball is struck. The goalkeeper must stand on his line without moving his feet until the ball is struck by an opponent, who cannot touch the ball again until someone else has done so.

Corner Kicks

If the ball crosses a team's goal-line between the goal and the side-lines having last been played by a member of the defending team, a corner kick is awarded. This is a direct free kick by the attacking team from the corner quarter-circle.

Throw-ins

If the ball crosses the side-lines, possession goes to the team opposite to that whose player last touched it. It must be returned into play from the point at which it crossed the line, being thrown with both hands and delivered from behind and over the head. Both feet of the thrower must be on or behind the side-line. Goals cannot be scored from throw-ins, nor can players be offside from a throw-in.

The Off-Side Law

A player is off-side if he is in the opposing half of the field and there are less than two players anywhere on the pitch between him and the goal at the moment a pass is struck by a team-mate. Since the goalkeeper rarely moves far from his goal, this means in effect that you are offside unless there is a defender between you and the goal. Being level with the player is not deemed to be offside.

Fig 2   The throw-in must be made with both feet behind the line, and the ball released by both hands from behind the head.

Fig 3   The attackers are played on side by the right back, who has not
followed his colleagues up the pitch.

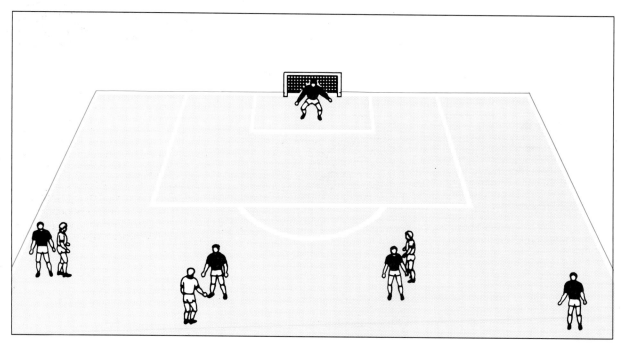

Fig 4   Level means on side, so this attacker has got it right.

Fig 5   *Referees do a difficult job and so deserve respect.*

Etiquette

The standard of behaviour of football players during matches is not always as high as the game deserves. All players must understand that the referee's decision is final, whether he be a qualified official or a colleague roped in to do the job. His authority should not be questioned and he should always be addressed with respect and politeness;

RULES CHECK

Once a player has been booked for an offence, committing another bookable offence allows the referee to send the player off the field of play, and he can take no further part in the match.

in other words you should always do as he says.

Equally, the players in the opposition team should be treated as people. Soccer is a contact sport in which aggression plays a part, but it should never degenerate into unnecessary contact or verbal insults. The ideal of the game is friendly and fair competition, in which both sides will do all they legally can to win. Shaking hands with opponents after a match is not just a ritual, it symbolizes the spirit of friendliness which should underline every soccer match.

CHAPTER 2

EQUIPMENT

Boots

The most important equipment for any soccer player is his pair of boots. He can play in a tight shirt, baggy shorts and odd socks without it affecting his performance, but the boots really do matter.

The boots must be comfortable. In the shop try them on while wearing soccer socks so that you get a proper idea of how tight or loose the boots are. Never buy boots a size bigger to grow into – this prevents you from getting a good feel for the ball and besides, the leather will rub and cause painful blisters. Make sure that the outer edges of the boots are well padded to prevent chaffing, and that the tongue is wide enough to keep out moisture (this is one area some boot manufacturers have been known to economize on).

Soccer boots have studs to give grip on soft surfaces. As these surfaces are bound to vary through the season, you have the choice of a pair of boots which seem to offer a reasonable compromise between the long studs needed in very wet conditions, or of the shorter kind required on harder ground. Alternatively you could buy boots which take screw-in studs, allowing you to choose from a range of studs according to your preference. The drawback, however, is that screw-in studs can loosen if not fitted properly, and once one stud is lost you will struggle to keep good balance. Screw-in studs can also inflict blisters if used when playing on clay-type surfaces. On the whole it is less trouble and perfectly sensible to opt for a boot with moulded rubber or plastic studs.

Laces should be firmly tied, going under the foot if possible, and bows should be tucked inside the boot to prevent them catching on another player's studs during a game.

Referees commonly check players' boots to ensure no metal is showing through the studs, as this obviously can cause injury to others. The complications that would follow if you were found to be wearing illegal boots are obvious, and you should check them yourself a few days before each match to give you time to repair any faults.

The leather in the boots will soften with use, but initially you may find it useful to smear petroleum jelly on the inside toe and heel areas to prevent rubbing. If the boots still rub, try sticking a plaster on the part of the boot which is causing the problem.

After use, scrape as much mud as you can from the boots with a blunt knife, then take off the rest with a brush or cloth (an old toothbrush might do the trick). If the boots are very wet, pack newspaper inside them to prevent shrinkage as the moisture dries out. Do not dry boots by a fire or in an airing cupboard as the leather will crack. Once dry, treat them with a water-resistant wax coating or, at the very least, with shoe polish – anything to nourish and soften the leather. It is much better to do this as soon as the boots are dry rather than at the last minute before your next match!

It is advisable to train while wearing your football boots too, as this will improve your feel of the ball. Often there is the temptation to wear some kind of sports shoe, but these often have very thin uppers which do not protect the toes and instep. The exception to this rule is when you play on concrete or very hard surfaces. Here training shoes are much better. If you are playing on a synthetic (plastic) surface, you should use special boots which have a high number of small studs to give a good grip on this difficult surface.

Shin Pads

Shin pads provide protection against bruises or worse injuries on a very vulnerable and sensitive part of the body. It is advisable for players to get used to wearing them in training as well as during matches. There is an excellent range of lightweight, shaped pads on the market which can be taped or tied round the shin. Some are moulded to protect the ankles, too. All professionals use shin pads, because they know it may help them continue their careers, and some even wear shin pads on the backs of their legs to protect their calves! It is foolhardy to allow youngsters to avoid wearing shin pads thus risking serious damage to young limbs.

Players who are concerned about damaging their ankles may also choose to wear an ankle sock or a bandage around the area. This is perfectly acceptable and such bandages can prevent a twisted ankle, especially when the game is played on a hard surface.

Socks

These should be clean and without holes to help avoid rubbing and blisters. Ideally, socks (or at least the section around the feet) should be made of cotton. This allows moisture out, so stopping potential fungal infections. Tie a thin length of bandage around the top to keep socks up round your calves. Do not use elastic as this can restrict blood circulation if it is too tight.

Training Clothes

It is far better to be too hot than cold during training sessions, which by necessity

Fig 6   Cones are very useful pieces of equipment in training.

sometimes grind to a halt while a point is being explained. Players should wear track suits which should be waterproof in wet weather.

KIT CHECK

For players trying to lose weight, plastic clothing worn during a training session makes the body sweat more and can help to shed a few pounds.

It is also always useful to have a stock of coloured vests to be worn over other clothes to differentiate players when the squad is divided into teams for a practice match or session.

Other Equipment

Petroleum jelly rubbed over the legs helps keep muscles warm, and every coach should be equipped with a selection of bandages, plasters, water bottles, pain-killing sprays and so on. The pain-killing sprays should be used with caution, however, especially with young teams as they dull the pain of an injury, but do not cure it. A damaged muscle will suffer further from stress if it is used throughout a match, even if the player feels no pain.

Some football clubs use small, portable goals for training sessions. These are about the size of a hockey goal, and more in proportion for small-scale practice games. However, goalkeepers should be discouraged from using them as they will

suffer disorientation once back in a normal-sized goal.

KIT CHECK

Cones like those used for traffic control are excellent props as obstacles or goals in training sessions. Any portable cone or pot will do.

Cones of the type used in traffic control are excellent items of equipment for training. They can act as obstacles, targets, or simply be used to mark out an area or indicate a line. They are also easily stackable so do not occupy too much storage space.

PART 2

SKILLS AND TECHNIQUES

CHAPTER 3

WHAT IS SKILL?

In soccer, as in any other game, enthusiasm and enjoyment are not enough for fulfilment or success; you also need skill. Ironically, the more naturally talented a player is, the less incentive he will have to work on improving his technique – and he will suffer for that later on. Any soccer player in today's highly flexible game must have an array of skills. It is not enough to be a superb dribbler; you must be able to pass the ball, to shoot, to head the ball, to get back and cover an opponent, and to tackle. The able defender must learn to pass accurately, to support team-mates in attack, and perhaps to strike an unstoppable penalty.

The aim is not to create a set of all-rounders with the same set of skills, but to develop every player to his full potential. That can only be done from a sound foundation of the basic skills of the game: controlling and passing the ball. From there, a player can build on his own preferred skills, related to the position he plays, but in doing this, care should be taken to achieve a balance of skills.

The simplest analogy is that of favourite feet. Most players have a best and a second-best foot – the one they prefer to shoot or pass from, and the other. However, those keen to improve their game work hard at improving their skills with both feet so that they do not become predictable and limited in what they can do on the pitch.

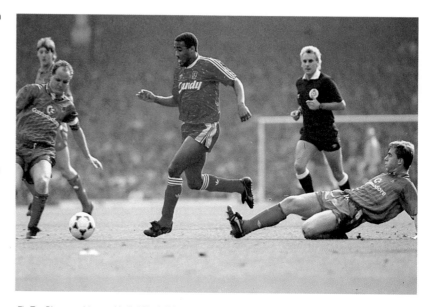

Fig 7   Players with good ball skills delight spectators and terrify opponents. John Barnes is a prime example.

Now if you substitute 'attack' and 'defence' for 'best foot' and 'second-best' in that statement, you will see that a good soccer player works not only to use both feet, but to play in both styles – getting the ball, then using it. Some national teams insist on players in the squad playing out of position in practice games. The aim of this is partly to test and develop their skills, and also to build up an awareness of what it is like to face a fast dribbler, compete for a header against a tall defender, or whatever.

Players can work on their skills both individually and together. Watching other people play is an excellent way to pick up tips or spot techniques you could learn yourself. However talented you are, there is always more to learn – that is one of the joys of the game.

CHAPTER 4

CONTROL

You can't be a good footballer without excellent ball control skills. From receiving passes to making interceptions, or just getting into a position to have a shot at goal, the first touch is a key element in your game. Good technique at this essential skill provides the confidence to attempt to do something positive with the ball.

RULES CHECK

Carrying, striking or propelling the ball with the hand or arm is a foul. Spread arms will help keep you balanced and avoid violating this law, which is punished by a direct free kick.

Once they have controlled the ball, players do one of three things: screen it; strike it for a pass or shot; or dribble it. The first touch determines how well they are going to be able to do any of these things quickly. The most common first sign of good technique is a player who gets into the line of flight of the ball, so that he is balanced and poised at the moment of contact. So you must select early on where and how you are going to control the ball, and adjust your position and body accordingly.

Trapping the Ball

In tight situations where you are closely marked or need time to see where other players are moving, trapping the ball by killing it dead is the required skill. Ironically, this movement can make more time than a quick turn, because very often it is the last thing your marker is expecting you to do, especially if you have been keeping him busy by constant movement.

Fig 8   Trapping the ball with the side of the foot.

The Basics

As the ball touches the ground, lower the foot on to the ball, pegging it to the ground. Keep the body balanced and steady.

Improving Your Skills

Lean into the trapping action so that your whole body moves over the ball. Learn a more sensitive touch with the sole and either side of the boot so that you can roll the ball to a better position straight after receiving it. This will help you to shield it from your marker and give you time to

glance up to assess the possibilities for passing.

Exercises

1.   Throw the ball in the air and trap it on its return. Practise the trapping technique after the ball has bounced before moving on to trying to trap it as it falls.
2.   Practise trapping returns from throw-ins against a wall.
3.   Put two players in the centre circle and ask one to throw the ball at the other's feet at angles and paces that will be difficult to control. Make the practice competitive by keeping a score of how often each fails to trap the other's throw.

KEY POINT: PITFALLS

Attackers and midfielders tend to have better instinctive ball control than defenders, so it is important for defending players in particular to work on their ball control, especially if they intend to enjoy a role in supporting the attack as well.

Using the Instep

The Basics

Keep balanced, move one foot so it is close underneath the ball, and use the other foot to absorb the bounce and kill the ball. Retain your balance so that you can move in any direction.

Improving Your Skills

The body, and in particular the foot, has to be relaxed and not tense or rigid, so that it can quickly and accurately be positioned

Fig 9   Balance and touch combine when controlling a falling ball with the instep.

Fig 10   When taking a pass from the side, lean into the flight of the ball to give the controlling movement some forward momentum.

and can absorb the impact of the ball. Try to make that first touch on the ball last as long as possible – the longer your boot is in contact with the ball, the more pace you are able to take off it and the more control you are able to exercise. The foot needs to travel at the same speed as the ball if it is to take off the pace and it must swing from the knee to build that pace. It may be helpful for you to view this movement as a follow-through in reverse.

Exercises

1.   Strike the ball firmly against a wall and move to attack and control it. You should then hit the ball back at the wall at an angle so that you have to move to receive it again.
2.   Players are paired up 10–15 yd (9–14m) from each other. The first passes the ball quite hard to his partner, who controls it with his instep, and with his next touch returns the ball. The foot used for both the control and the return pass should be alternated.

Outside of the Foot

Basics

To maintain your balance when controlling the ball with the outside of the foot you must lean your body in the direction from which the ball is coming. Again, the foot must absorb the pace of the ball to retain control.

Improving Your Skills

The outstep is invaluable for controlling the ball and turning at the same time, doing little more than deflecting the ball and allowing you to steer it into space, away from your marker.

Keep your supporting leg between your opponent and the ball, as this will help you to keep your balance and screen the ball from him. Spread your arms for better balance, and keep your foot very relaxed so that it can absorb the impact of the ball while the rest of the body is making the first move of the turn, sprint or whatever. Few players are capable of using either

outstep to control the ball well, yet defenders in particular can use this technique on many occasions in a match.

Exercises

1.   Use a wall to collect rebound passes as in the previous exercise, using only the outside of the boot.
2.   Position one player at the penalty spot and another in the goal. The outfield player plays the ball along the ground towards the goal, while his colleague must use the outside of his foot to control the ball. The goal-line prevents him retreating to make the action easier and instills the idea of attacking the ball.

Using the Thigh

The thigh is underused for controlling the ball, yet in a match not all passes are played along the ground, so for receiving or intercepting – especially when you are on the move or the ball is dropping at you – the thigh can be invaluable.

Fig 11   The thigh trap: note the backwards lean balanced by the arms.

The Basics

Turn your whole body towards the ball, and ensure your supporting leg is slightly bent as the ball lands on your thigh.

Improving Your Skills

As with the outstep, few players are adept at using either thigh to welcome the ball. Experiment with using different degrees of knee bend to allow the thigh to accept the ball at varying angles. Remember that the thigh is one of the least vulnerable places when used to control the ball – defenders find it much harder to attack than the feet, for example.

Exercises

1.   Throw the ball about 15ft (4.5m) in the air and control it with your thigh after it has bounced once. When you are proficient at this, take the ball as it falls without allowing it to hit the ground.

2.   Strike the ball high on to a wall, and control the rebound with the thigh, practising both pushing the ball up to volley it at the wall again, and cushioning it to strike it from the ground. Make sure you do not retreat from the wall – try to stand closer than your instincts tell you and you will be training yourself to attack the ball and get there first.

3.   Two players can practise throw-ins which are to be controlled on the thigh – either direct or on the first bounce.

Using the Chest and Shoulders

Footballers usually have well-developed thighs with plenty of flesh to soften the blow of the ball and stop it bounding away. Their chests tend to be less developed and anyway are a harder, less flexible surface. You must therefore use your whole body to receive the ball on your chest or shoulders.

Fig 12   Chest control requires the use of the whole body which must be balanced and turned to the line of flight. Note the bent knees and extended arms as the chest prepares to absorb the impact of the ball.

Fig 13   Fooling an international defender takes guile, nerve and superb ball control. Here England's Chris Waddle is in total command as he beats a Swedish player.

The Basics

Angle your body upwards as the ball approaches and on impact turn it down to take the pace off the ball.

Improving Your Technique

Balls at this height are usually travelling quite fast, and players facing them tend to flex and tense their muscles, presenting a hard wall from which the ball is bound to ricochet. Instead, drop your arms to the side, relax your wrists (which makes the rest of the upper body less tense) and breathe easily and calmly.

> **KIT CHECK**
>
> Controlling the ball requires flexibility, and even if your joints are made of rubber, you can't be flexible if your kit is too tight. Borrowed, shrunken or simply old kit can cramp your body and your style. Make sure you can move all your joints freely inside your kits.

Once you have mastered the technique, you can afford to relearn bad, old habits and use the tense, rigid chest for passing. This is likely to surprise and hence unsettle defences and is an excellent way of pushing the ball rapidly into the danger area behind defenders for an on-rushing colleague. To do this, twist the trunk from the hips to change the direction of the ball. The tense chest can also be used to control a ball which is bouncing upwards. Stoop over the ball and let it rebound down so that it can be controlled on the ground.

Exercises

1.   Use the wall and pairs technique described previously, with the ball being controlled at chest height.
2.   For the more advanced chest pass, start with two players quite close together, one throwing the ball and running for the

Fig 14   The chest can control a rising ball, too, if the whole body is bent over the ball.

Fig 15   The chest can be used instead of a header to control quite high balls and it offers better ball protection.

Fig 16   *West German midfielder Thomas Haessler is poised, balanced and has the ball totally under control, his body low over it.*

return chest pass. When the players become more proficient (and this will take some time) put a defender on the player who is using his chest so that he has the feeling of using the technique under pressure.

Shielding the Ball

The Basics

Keep your body between your opponent and the ball.

Improving Your Technique

Although the principle of using your body to protect the ball stands at all times, you do not have to be in this position constantly: you only need to protect the ball at moments when you may be vulnerable to attack. Furthermore, if your control technique is good, you need not use your whole body to shield the ball, but instead you can keep the ball on the outside foot, for example, giving the defender little chance of reaching it.

Figs 18 (a)–(c)   Shielding the ball.

Fig 18 (a)   When receiving under pressure, move towards the ball.

Fig 17   While the body shields the ball, your mind can choose your next move, or wait for the defender to commit himself: ball protection gives you time to think.

Exercises

1.   In a 15yd (14m) area, get one player to pass the ball towards two others, who compete to control it, and who must then protect it for 5 seconds (counted out loud by the original passer) before moving away and playing the ball to the other two players to attack, and so on.
2.   Set up a row of cones 2yd (2m) apart, and get players to dribble the ball through them using only the outside of the boot, alternating feet after every cone. This practises moving with a shielded ball.

Protection through Movement

The defender will be expecting you to try to move with the ball, indeed he will probably be encouraging you to move in a certain direction, away from the danger area. Actual movement will be covered in

Fig 18 (b)   Control it while your body shields it from your marker.

Fig 18 (c)   Get the ball down on to the ground as quickly as possible.

the section on dribbling, but feinting to move is an excellent ball protection and space creation technique.

Exercise

Players can practise dummies on their own with a moving or stationary ball, making sudden movements to either side, swinging the leg over or round the ball, but hardly touching it. They can then pair up to attack one another, and will learn that

even when you know the ball holder is not going to take the ball with him, his movements are enough to keep you off the ball.

Shielding the Ball out of Play

Defenders often find a stray pass or deflected ball coming towards or past them. Provided an opposition player

struck it last and that the ball is heading out of play, the defender will gain more time if he lets the ball run off the pitch and wins a throw-in or goal kick. He must track the ball and shield it from any opponents, however, by keeping his body between the ball and the attacker. This is not necessarily done by running in a straight line behind the ball – attackers may be able to slide round the defender. A zig-zagging run, jostling around the ball offers better protection.

CHAPTER 5

PASSING

Passing is the life-blood of team play, and is the ball-playing action made most often by players during a match. Accuracy is obviously the prime requirement, but to be precise when playing the ball you have to know why it is going in that direction, so you must be aware of your colleague's positions and of the match tactics being used.

Throughout the following exercises, try not to think of passing as an end in itself; releasing the ball gives you an opportunity to move into space or to support a colleague, perhaps to regain the ball. 'Pass and move' is a simple phrase on which many teams base their match play.

The Push Pass

The push pass is the most accurate way of getting the ball to a colleague, as it presents a large area of the boot to the ball.

The Basics

The non-kicking foot is placed next to the ball, and the body is over the ball on point of impact. Contact is with the inside of the

Fig 20 For the push pass, get the supporting foot as near as possible to the ball, and aim to make contact just below the middle line.

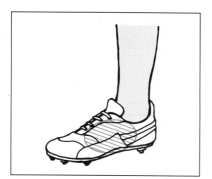

Fig 19 The area of the foot used to hit the side-foot pass.

boot at right angles to the line of the pass, with the leg being swung from the hip.

Improving Your Technique

Contact should be through the horizontal mid-line of the ball to ensure the pass stays low. Keep your eyes on the ball, with your head still down as the pass is played. The non-kicking foot can be kept to one side to allow room for the kicking leg to swing.

Exercises

1. Push passes should be practised with two players in a 10yd (9m) square, being played first to feet and then to one side to encourage the idea of moving to meet the ball. Players should take one touch to control the ball, and pass back with the second. As they become more familiar with the pass, both players should begin to move all the time during this exercise to force the other to look up and find his man.

2. Position one player 15yd (14m) from two others, and get him to push pass the ball towards them. One runs to control and return it, and it is played again for the second player, only this time the passer follows the ball to take up the position first occupied by the pair. Thus the practice of moving to the ball, passing and moving again is sustained.

The trouble with the push pass is that its careful action makes the pass predictable, it lacks power over long distances and is tricky to make when running at speed. However, there are numerous other types of pass which can be used as well.

Passing with the Instep

The Basics

Since a smaller part of the boot is in contact with the ball, the driven pass with the instep is a more difficult skill than the push pass. Again, the body must be balanced and over the ball at impact, but a certain amount of lean is allowed to give the leg room to swing and perhaps lift the ball slightly.

Improving Your Technique

The ball is struck with the toe pointing at a downwards angle so that contact is through the vertical line of the ball. The approach should be at an angle of about 30 degrees.

Exercises

1.   Use a wall with targets marked on it to learn to strike the ball accurately.
2.   In a 30yd (27m) square, get two players to drive the ball first at each other and then into space towards which the receiver is moving.

Fig 22   Spread the arms to give better balance for the volley pass with the instep.

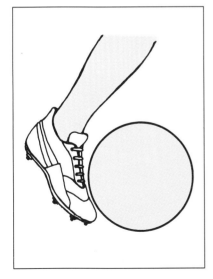

Fig 21   The angle of contact for the driven pass with the instep.

> **STAR TIP**
>
> I have to get quite a lot of whipped power on to the ball, so I use the instep and top of my foot and very little backswing. But to get the direction and height right is very difficult.
>   Brian Marwood [on corner kicks]
>   *Inside Football*, 13, 1990.

The Lofted Pass

The Basics

The lofted pass is made in a similar way to the driven pass except that the supporting foot is further from the ball and contact is made with a scooping action under the ball to lift it.

Fig 23   For the lofted pass with the instep, the body leans back but the ball is struck firmly and not scooped.

Improving Your Technique

The kicking foot is opened out more, and there should be a smooth follow-through to maintain accuracy. The ankle should be firm, and the body should be leaning slightly back. By taking a wider angle of approach some back-spin is imparted, slowing the pace of the ball after the bounce.

Exercise

Two players 40yd (37m) apart exchange passes over the head of a defender who cannot move closer than 15yd (14m) to them. If only two players are available, use the goal as an obstacle area over which to loft the ball.

The Chip

The Basics

The supporting foot is kept close to the ball, and the kicking leg is held straight, with

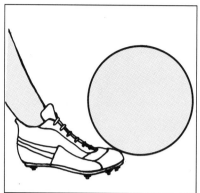

Fig 24   For the chip, the ball is struck on the underside with a stabbing movement.

a stabbing contact made with the underside of the ball.

Improving Your Technique

The approach to the ball should be straight. It is easier to chip a ball rolling towards you than to chip a dead ball. Accuracy is the element to work on, both in where the ball lands, and its trajectory – this is important to ensure that you lift the ball over your opponents.

Fig 25   To chip the ball, contact with the ball must be at the lowest possible point, and the supporting foot must be close by to angle the swing of the striking leg correctly.

Exercises

1.   Stand players on the edge of the centre circle, with one player on the centre spot. Ask the players to chip the ball over the solitary player so that they land as near as possible to the centre circle line opposite.
2.   Position two players 25yd (23m) apart, each with a ball. They should simultaneously chip to each other over a colleague, control the incoming ball, and repeat the process. This will build up accuracy and speed of thought in controlling and passing the ball.

Using the Outside of the Foot

The Basics

The kicking foot moves across the body to strike the ball with a glancing blow or flick.

Improving Your Technique

Using the outside of the boot for a front

Fig 26   The pass with the outside of the boot is hit across the ball.

Fig 27   The front foot pass allows you to play the ball without coming under pressure, even when an opponent is in close attendance.

foot pass which is struck in full stride, saves a yard and surprises opponents. It is a very quick way of getting the ball a fair distance away, and was perhaps best demonstrated by the attacking German sweeper Franz Beckenbauer.

Exercise

In an area 40yd by 10yd (37m by 9m), get players to use the outside of the boot to hit a moving ball to each other. Eventually you can add defenders who should shadow them without challenging – this will give the feeling of carrying out the move under pressure.

RULES CHECK

A colleague is off-side if there are less than two opponents between him and the opposing goal-line the moment a pass is hit. So passes to players on the front line are better hit early than late if the defence is moving up.

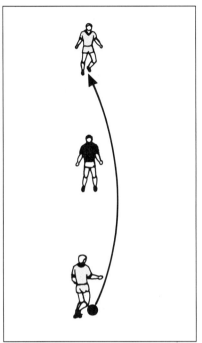

Fig 28   Passes can be curled around a defender with the swerving pass.

The Swerving Pass

The Basics

The ball is struck with a glancing blow to impart side-spin which will curl it around defenders between passer and receiver.

Improving Your Technique

The swerve on the ball can be used not only to avoid defenders but to bring the ball into the path of a moving player. The receiver must be aware that the ball is spinning so that he can judge the bounce variation. The firmer the strike, the longer it takes for the curve to establish itself.

Exercises

1.   A sliced pass against a wall will rebound at an angle, back towards where it was struck. This is good basic, initial practice.

2.   In a 40yd by 10yd (37m by 9m) area, players at each end bend the ball around a defender who is positioned in the middle.
3.   In a 40yd square (37m square) area, players strike curling passes into space. Their colleague must run on to the ball and judge the bounce so that they can take the ball without breaking stride. When they are proficient at this, a defender can be added and who must be beaten by the pass.

KEY POINT: COMMON FAULTS

For defenders, playing the ball back to the goalkeeper (the 'back pass') is often the safest option. This pass should only be attempted if you have the goalkeeper in your field of view or have heard his call. Whenever possible, a back pass should be steered to one side of the goal, to avoid the danger of scoring an own goal if the goalkeeper misses the ball.

The Wall Pass

The Basics

The wall pass, or 'one two', is a simple return pass to a player who has moved into space. The ball movement usually describes a triangle shape with a defender stranded in its middle.

Improving Your Technique

Always try to play the return ball with the outside leg, so that the widest possible angle is put on the pass. Many players restrict themselves to playing the wall pass only when they are near the opposing penalty area. Yet it is such an effective and safe way of retaining possession while moving the ball that it should be used anywhere on the pitch, including in defensive positions.

Exercises

1.   Set cones in a row about 3yd (3m)

Figs 29 (a)–(c)   The wall pass.

Fig 29 (a)   The wall pass is the classic way for two players to defeat one. The ball is played out of range of the defender to a colleague.

Fig 29 (b)   The colleague uses his outside foot to return it into the path of the original passer.

Fig 29 (c)   The original passer has moved blind side of the defender, leaving him stranded.

apart. Players perform a series of wall passes, imagining the cones are defenders.
2.   Play a five-a-side game in which goals can only be scored directly after wall passes.

The Back-Heel Pass

The Basics

The ball is struck with the back of the heel, the supporting leg being close by the ball, and the body balanced and ready to move away.

Improving Your Technique

Since the ball is struck with a narrow part of the boot, accuracy needs to be worked on. You can also work on using the sole of the boot for a slower, but more accurate pass. The technique can be developed into a sideways flick from behind, with the body pushing the ball square rather than backwards.

KEY POINT: PITFALLS

The back-heel is an excellent way of disconcerting defenders but it relies on awareness of other players' positions and the use of runs into the path of the back-heeled ball.

Exercises

1.   Back-heel the ball against a wall. Control the rebound and repeat.
2.   Set two players off to run the length of the pitch, one moving ahead of the other and back-heeling the ball into his colleague's path. The receiver sprints ahead with the ball and repeats the pattern.

The Volley Pass

Striking the ball while it is in the air has the advantages of speed and surprise.

Fig 30 When back-heeling, aim to strike the middle of the ball with as much of your heel as possible to maintain accuracy. Get the supporting leg close to the ball.

Fig 31 The sole of the boot is used for slower, more accurate passes behind you.

The Basics

Position your supporting leg so it is parallel to the line of the ball, and keep your knee above the ball to give maximum control on pace and direction.

Improving Your Technique

The ball should not be struck on its underside, but through its vertical mid-line and in the bottom half. The ankle should be extended. To hook the ball, position yourself side on to the line of the ball. If you are striking the ball high up, you can be further from it than if you are hitting it just above ground level.

Exercises

1. A wall makes an ideal 'partner' for volley practice. Aim for specific targets and

angles in your volleys. Make sure you alternate the foot being used in order to widen the range of your skills.

2.   Players 25yd (23m) apart should volley to each other, calling out 'facing' or 'side on' as they pass so that their colleague receives an instruction on how to treat the ball.

Crossing

A cross is a pass, usually into the penalty area, which is likely to result in an attempt on goal. Awareness of your team-mates' positions and preferences for types of cross, and accuracy in delivering the ball, are vital.

The question of where to play the cross is dealt with in Chapter 13. The main point as far as crossing skills are concerned is that with the freedom of movement many players enjoy, from roaming strikers to overlapping full backs, just about every player in the team needs to be adept at crossing the ball.

The High Cross

The basics

The underside of the ball is struck by the instep, with the kicking action being across the body. Pivot on the supporting leg with the body leaning back.

Improving Your Technique

A burst of acceleration as you are about to strike the ball helps get past the defender and builds momentum for striking the cross. A glancing blow on the ball will impart side-spin, which is useful for swerving the ball away from goalkeepers and into the path of attackers. Spread the arms for greater balance.

Exercises

1.   Since crosses are generally directed into space in front of attackers, the best training is to take the ball down the touch-line with a colleague running into the middle. By glancing up or exchanging calls, you should be able to time your cross (from the edge of the area or byline) to meet his run. When you find this exercise easy, try adding a goalkeeper and then a tracking defender.

On set pieces such as corners and free kicks; the aim sometimes is to hit to a static target man who will head the ball on. Since he will be able to jump to a height equivalent to that of the goal (8ft or 2.5m), hang some track suits from the bar as targets and try to hit them with lofted crosses. The low driven cross is hit as the driven pass, as are other types of cross such as the chip.

Fig 33   (Opposite) John Barnes of England is one of the great crossers of the ball. He can follow a trick and burst of speed as seen here with a pin-point pass, without breaking stride.

Figs 32 (a)–(d)   Crossing.

Fig 32 (a)   A burst of pace can often provide space in which to make a cross. The winger flicks the ball outside the defender as he commits himself.

Fig 32 (b)   The winger accelerates past the defender into space.

Check Out Receipt

Thomas Library
219-926-7696

Monday, May 5 2014 7:30PM

Title: Soccer for dummies
Due: 06/02/2014

Title: The World Cup : the complete hist
ory
Due: 06/02/2014

Title: Soccer : technique, tactics, trai
ning
Due: 06/02/2014

Items must be returned to the library
and checked in before closing on the
date(s) due.
Thank you!

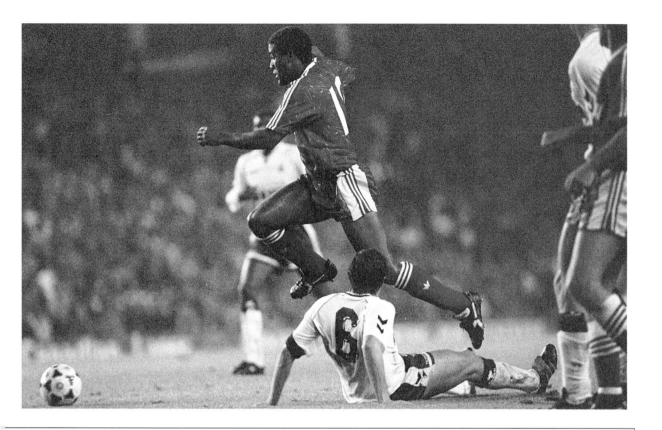

Fig 32 (c)　　The winger then has time for a quick glance up.

Fig 32 (d)　　The winger makes the cross.

Figs 34 (a)–(c)   Throw-ins.

Fig 34 (a)   Build up pace and momentum for the long throw with a sprint.

Fig 34 (b)   Spread the legs for the throw.

Fig 34 (c)   Swing the arms forcefully through to transfer all that effort into the ball.

Throw-ins

The Basics

A good long throw can be as effective as a corner, but the technique requires some work. Keep both feet on the ground, and

> **STAR TIP**
>
> I keep both feet firmly on the ground and do a standing throw. I stand still with my feet close to the line and bend my back. In my style you get the momentum and power from the swing of your torso.
> Gary Mabbutt [on an alternative approach to the long throw]
> *Inside Football*, 9, 1990.

do not step on to the pitch until the ball is released. You throw with the back as much as with the arms, so develop a whiplash movement and a strong follow-through for extra power. A medicine ball is the ideal piece of equipment with which to practice with.

CHAPTER 6

HEADING

Heading is one of the hardest skills to learn in soccer because it requires such good timing to meet the ball in the air at the optimum moment ahead of a challenger, and to direct the ball where you want it to go.

> **RULES CHECK**
>
> Soccer is a contact sport and you should not wear jewellery such as wrist watches, necklaces or bracelets, which could injure another player if you should collide.

But every player (even the goalkeeper sometimes) needs to be able to meet the ball in the air confidently with his head, as the ball spends more time in the air than on the ground in some games.

Beginners at heading often have three faults: they are afraid the ball will hurt; they shut their eyes on impact with the ball; and they make contact with the top of the head instead of the forehead. To counteract this, hang some footballs from the goal bar in plastic bags or nets. Ask players to head these balls around gently to get them used to the contact of ball with forehead. Next, start them practising on the softest (but not easiest) of headers: the controlling header.

> **STAR TIP**
>
> If a fiercely hit ball is coming at you and you want to head it clear, don't let the ball hit you – you must attack the ball. Keep your eyes open and push your forehead into the ball.
>
> Bryan Robson
>
> Robson, B. *Soccer Skills* (Hamlyn, 1987).

The Controlling Header

The Basics

Cushion the ball on the forehead by relaxing the neck muscles and keeping your eyes on the ball.

Improving Your Technique

If your whole body is relaxed from toes to head, it will be better equipped for the header. Get up on your toes with your knees bent, and lean your body back as the ball approaches.

> **KEY POINT: PITFALLS**
>
> You should avoid heading the ball while you are travelling backwards – you will not be able to generate sufficient power or control with your header. Positioning and timing are as important as the actual heading technique.

Exercises

1. Stand two players 5yd (4.5m) apart and get one to throw the ball in a gentle arc for the other to control on his head, and pass back on the ground. Build on this exercise by having the ball thrown at varying angles so that the receiver has to move to the side or back to take the ball on his head.
2. Line players up on the edge of the penalty area. From the six-yard line, balls are thrown gently towards the penalty spot. Players take turns to meet the ball with a controlling header and shooting for goal.

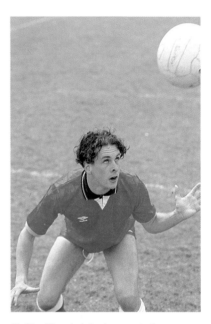

Fig 35 *The whole body supports the controlling header like a shock absorber. Note the total concentration of eye on ball.*

3. Juggling the ball on the head is superb practice. The practice can be made competitive by keeping a count of how many touches each player can make or how long each player can keep the ball in the air using his head.
4. Place a player on the six-yard line and another just outside the penalty area. The latter should try to chip the ball into the net, while the defender is forced to use his head to control the ball before passing it back.

Fig 36 (Overleaf) *Good attacking heading requires positional skills, courage, and the use of the whole body. Gary Lineker shows how it is done.*

Defensive Headers

The Basics

Aim to meet the twin objectives of getting to the ball first and clearing it from the danger area. The jump should be timed so that you reach the ball at the earliest opportunity, and your header should push the ball up and away.

Improving Your Technique

Timing your header is a tricky blend of watching the ball and your opponent. You must ensure that you get there first without being under so much pressure that you cannot make a clean header. When the ball is falling or hanging, your head will move to watch its flight, so the ball is more likely to hit the forehead and rebound upwards – but not under control. Instead, keep away from the ball until you can attack it, and then swing your trunk as you go to head the ball, leaning into the header.

Exercises

1. Use a rugby pitch and position someone behind the touch-line to send over crosses towards the area in front of the posts. You must head the ball over the bar. The angle of delivery from behind the touch-line reproduces the most likely angle at which crosses will reach you.
2. Head tennis, in which the football can only bounce once, is an excellent game for improving power and directional control in heading. It is played to the rules of tennis, either on a tennis court or in the gym.

Fig 37 (a)   Defensive heading is all about balancing the best time to head the ball accurately against the necessity of stopping the attacker reaching the cross first. The defender gets in first having correctly judged that the pair ahead of him would not reach the cross.

Fig 37 (b)   His whole trunk has helped project the ball up and away.

Fig 37 (c)   This has eliminated the danger.

Figs 37 (a)–(c)   Defensive headers.

(a)

(b)

(c)

Attacking Headers

The Basics

Put lots of power into your header by striking the ball from above with the meat of the forehead and driving it downwards towards the goal. Goalkeepers have most difficulty reaching balls from this angle.

Improving Your Technique

When heading for goal from crosses, use the shooting rule of striking the ball back towards the direction from which it came. So, if the cross is from the right of the goal, head towards the right post – the goalkeeper will be moving the other way to follow the ball. Although it is generally best to head the ball from above, any contact which is made before a defender can reach the ball will change the direction of flight and may produce a chance for a colleague. You should therefore get to the ball early and spread your arms for balance and protection.

For jumps from a stationary position, you will need to use both legs to push you up. When you have more momentum, you should be able to jump from either foot, thus increasing your flexibility.

Exercises

1. Hanging a ball from the bar and striking it with the centre of the forehead, then heading it again as it swivels around, is excellent practice for improving your technique and reflexes.
2. Get a colleague to throw the ball at you from about 5yd (4.5m), and try to head it down past his feet – he will also get good training in ball control!

Fig 38 (a) With attacking headers, the emphasis is on getting there first and directing the ball down, with power being a secondary aim. The attacker has moved into the line of flight.

Fig 38 (b) The attacker glances the ball sideways and down.

Fig 38 (c) The ball is aimed just inside the post.

Figs 38 (a)–(c)   Attacking headers.

(a)

(b)

(c)

Figs 39 (a)–(c)   Heading for goal.

Fig 39 (a)   Heading for goal at the near post has the added advantage that the goalkeeper may be unsighted or out of position. Here the attacker makes a diagonal run to get there first.

Fig 39 (b)   The attacker's momentum adds power to the strike.

Fig 39 (c)   The strike will then beat the goalkeeper.

The Diving Header

The Basics

The diving header can be a spectacular and effective way of meeting low crosses which are flying across in front of you.

Keep watching the ball, throw yourself full length, and aim to make contact with the forehead, not the top of the skull.

Improving Your Technique

Throw your arms out in front, keeping them below the height of your shoulders. This will add momentum to your dive and help get your whole body behind the ball so that you can catapult it towards the net. A flick of the head as you make contact will help to direct it towards the desired corner, but wait until your technique has improved before you add this move. Use your relaxed arms to cushion your fall – and beware of any low flying boots in the area.

Exercises

1. Suspend a ball from the goal bar or in the gym at about waist height, with mattresses placed under it. Get players to make diving headers without waiting for the ball to settle between attempts. You could form two teams and compete for how many successful (in other words, fully struck) headers are made.
2. Using a small, wide pitch, set up games in which only goals scored with a diving header count. Vary the crosses from hard, low centres to more lofted balls that will bounce for the header.

STAR TIP

The thing about this type of header is that it happens very quickly. It's not like a normal header, where you have time to watch the flight of the ball and get above it . . . It is instinctive.

Keith Houchen [on diving headers]
Inside Football, 23, 1990.

Figs 40 (a)–(c)   The diving header.

Fig 40 (a)   The diving header drives the ball with the full weight and momentum of the body. Contact is made with the forehead, not the top of the head.

Fig 40 (b)   Landing is softened by the knees and bent elbows.

Fig 40 (c)   A safe and successful landing for body and ball!

Fig 41   Gary Stevens of England has his eye on the ball after making a controlled header under pressure.

Glancing Headers

The Basics

Once you have mastered the timing and balance of heading, you can start to use the head as a block from which the ball is allowed to bounce at controlled angles.

KEY POINT: PITFALLS

The harder a ball is struck, the more pace and power a glancing header from it will have. So any contact near the goal can be decisive.

Improving Your Technique

Whatever you are trying to do, the key point is the force behind the ball you are about to head. It has to be hit fairly hard to sustain pace after your intervention. The degree of contact and the angles achieved are largely a matter of experience.

Exercises

1.   Defenders positioned just in front of the goal-line should try to head incoming shots over the bar from at least two players who shoot rapidly one after the other.
2.   Three players must get the ball into the net without it touching the ground from a throw-in near the penalty box without kicking the ball. This can be extended to a full game in which the ball can be handled, thrown and headed, but never kicked.

Fig 42   For the glancing header or flick on, the merest touch off the top of the forehead is sufficient to take the ball over an opponent.

Redirecting the Ball

The Basics

Changing the direction of the ball requires an extra action in the heading movement. Contact is with the front side of the head, which is turned on impact to completely switch the ball's line of flight.

Improving Your Technique

Despite the fact that your head has to turn on impact, your eyes should remain on the ball at all times. However, you can afford

Fig 43   When redirecting the ball, for example at a near-post cross, the whole trunk is twisted at impact.

to twist the trunk and swing it sideways into the point of impact. More subtle deflections are possible with the back-flick off the forehead and above, or allowing the ball to skim the top of the head. The change in the ball's line of flight will create difficulties for the defence, and even a slight deflection can put a goalkeeper off-balance and achieve a goal.

Exercise

Two players compete to head goals from a series of crosses. Even though they are both heading for goal, they will put each other under pressure.

CHAPTER 7

DRIBBLING

Dribbling is just about any move through which you take the ball past an opponent, from a crisply-executed flick and turn to a long run through a whole defence. Dribbling skills are not confined to the wispy winger, and are required by all footballers. That said, there is an inevitable risk factor in dribbling and it should be kept to a minimum in the defending third of the field.

There are a number of elements to successful dribbling, and these are dealt with separately in the rest of this chapter.

Fig 44   The good dribbler keeps his body over the ball, spreads his arms for balance, and often appears to have the ball attached to his boots by the laces!

STAR TIP

Dribbling is not only about ball control, it is also about lightning reactions. I used to be able to do what Pelé could do, and that was knock the ball against defenders' legs as one of my ploys, because I could always react faster than them.

George Best
Inside Football, 29, 1990.

Close Control

The Basics

To take the ball past people and run with it at speed you need excellent close control – the ball should look as if it is glued to your boots. Lean over the ball and never let it stray further than 1 ft (30cm) from your boot.

Improving Your Technique

You must learn to use every part of each foot, while retaining your balance, poise and ability so that you can look around to see what opponent's and team-mates are up to.

Exercises

1.   Touch the ball across with the right foot, push it on with the outside of the left, touch inside with the left instep, push with the right outstep, and so on. You can then reverse the pattern and control with the outstep, push with the instep, and so on.
2.   Pass the ball repeatedly between your insteps with the ball slightly in front, level and slightly behind them – this will allow you to become comfortable with the ball wherever it is.
3.   Juggling the ball helps improve control and balance. Set individual targets for how many touches you can keep the ball in the air, how long you can juggle the ball, and the number of touches you can achieve juggling the ball for 1 minute. You should build the frequency of contact – this is vital for dribbling.

KEY POINT: PITFALLS

Just as some teams capable of highly cultivated football can be put off their stride by lowlier opponents, so the dribbler with an array of subtle feints and dummies can find he is wasted on some defenders – they did not spot the move and so they were not put off by it! It is worth trying out a range of moves early on in a game to assess moves which could be useful to concentrate on.

Turning

The Basics

From the simple change of direction to the extravagant dummy and sprint away, there are numerous types of turn, some of which will be described later in the exercises. The fundamental point is to trick your opponent into thinking you are going one way, as this will make the turn in the opposite direction more effective. Confidence, good technique and balance are the essential requirements.

Improving Your Technique

This is all down to practice and imagination. Once you have mastered one turn, try another – build variety into your game. You should also be able to carry out turns in either direction – if you are particularly good at a piece of trickery involving a back-heel with the right foot, try to achieve this with your left foot toc

Exercises

1. Draw the ball inside on the instep,

Figs 45 (a)–(d) Dribbling I.

Fig 45 (a)   A dummy and change of pace can wrong-foot a defender. The attacker gestures or even shouts.

Fig 45 (b)   This is followed by a flick to one side.

Fig 45 (c)   The attacker gives a burst of acceleration.

Fig 45 (d)   This takes him past his man.

then flick the ball forward with the outside of the same foot. After a while, switch to using the opposite foot for the push forward.

2.   Step over the ball with the right foot, or swing the whole leg in an arc around the ball, then use the outside of the left foot to change direction. You can double this 'scissors' movement by carrying it out with both legs before making contact with the ball.

3.   Even simple moves such as a straight switch of direction by striking the ball across your body with the instep are improved if you use the outside of the other boot instead.

4.   Dummy to go right, and use the right back heel to flick the ball left and ahead. This is harder to do than it sounds but it is very effective!

All these moves, and any variations of them, should be practised by a group of players inside the centre circle – the players must not touch each other. This builds awareness of where other people are as you make your moves. A call from the coach for a change of direction every so often will keep players' minds active, too.

Eventually, you will be ready to try these moves against defenders. Set up two small goals in a 20sq yd (18sq m) area, and match up pairs of players in order to test their skill at dribbling and turning techniques.

Figs 46 (a)–(d)   Dribbling II.

Fig 46 (a)   Force the defender to commit himself from a good position.

Fig 46 (b)   Swing a leg round the ball – this will confuse him.

Fig 46 (c)   You can then take the ball to the side he leaves open.

Fig 46 (d)   This will win valuable space.

Figs 47 (a)–(f)   Dribbling III.

Fig 47 (a)   Prepare for your turn.

Fig 47 (b)   The body shields the ball.

Fig 47 (c)   Swing the right leg over the ball while turning.

Fig 47 (d)   Flick the ball sideways with the outside of the right

Fig 47 (e)   The defender is tempted in.

Fig 47 (f)   You are already moving out of his path and past him.

Dribbling at Speed

The Basics

Once you are moving at speed with the ball, you must reduce the number of touches required to retain control in order to look up and assess your next move. You must, however, watch the ball each time you make contact with it.

Improving Your Technique

Keep your ankle relaxed. You don't have to be a fast runner to be able to pass defenders at speed – it is all a matter of adjusting your pace and being able to burst past them. The move should be combined with a swerve or change of direction to confuse the defender.

When faced with two defenders, the most vulnerable space is the area between them, because they will be unsure which of them should challenge you. Slow down a little and then burst through the gap. This

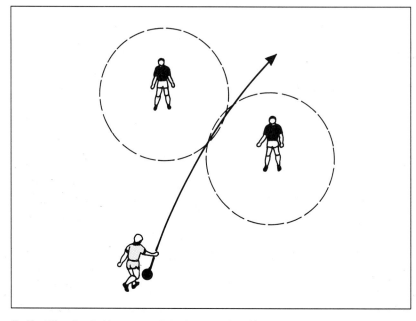

Fig 48   When faced with two opponents, the most vulnerable space to attack is the area between them – you will cause confusion about whose responsibility it is to attack.

was one of the favourite tricks of the great George Best.

Exercises

1.   Speed tends to be a natural asset and cannot be trained for, but speed off the mark can be improved upon through training.

Use narrow channels about 5yd (4.5m) wide and ask players to get past each other. Although this is of most benefit to the attacker, full-backs should try it too – they will then learn how their opponents think.

2.   Set up cones in a row 5yd (4.5m) apart and get players to run with the ball to the first, back to the starting line, then to the next, and so on. Add another player who approaches the cones from the other side to make a race of it and to add to the pressure at the turn.

CHAPTER 8

TACKLING

Tackling is not just a question of getting the ball back off an opponent. It requires timing and positional sense to know when to strike, and good technique to take the ball without fouling the player. There will be more guidance on the strategic timing of challenges and tackles in Part 3 on tactics.

Stance

Adopting a flexible stance from which to attack an opponent is fundamental to good defensive play.

The Basics

There are two kinds of stance: frontal, in which the defender faces square up to the attacker (good for moving sideways, but not for moving forward and back); and the diagonal stance in which the defender puts himself at an angle to the attacker, rather like a boxer. This allows him to move backwards and forwards more easily, but allows easy sideways movement to one side only.

Improving Your Technique

Defenders should decide which stance they prefer and work on it, rather than constantly switching between the two. The frontal stance is more natural for younger players as they can face their whole body towards the ball. However, the diagonal stance is more suitable for forcing a dribbler in a certain direction, or tracking back to contain an attacker. The key is to keep on your toes and be ready to react to your opponent's movements. The diagonal stance you take should turn your body in the same direction as that which the attacker is taking so that you can run with him without having to turn.

Exercise

In a 20 × 5yd (18 × 4.5m) corridor, attackers should try to beat defenders.

The latter should test out both stances until they are comfortable with one. The defender should then push the attacker towards one side as much as possible. He will have to adjust his stance and positioning in order to achieve this.

> **RULES CHECK**
>
> Succeeding in, or attempting to kick an opponent, tripping, charging from behind or in a dangerous manner, and pushing an opponent are all fouls punished by a direct free kick.

Positioning

The Basics

Positioning skills are vital as there are times when you do not necessarily need to tackle, but want to contain an attacker. The principle is that you decide when to

Fig 49   The frontal stance.

Fig 50   The angled stance is more crab-like and can be used to force an attacker one way.

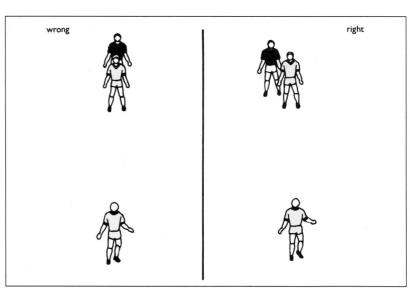

Fig 51   Stand at an angle to the man you are marking – you can see better and react faster.

tackle, and do not allow yourself to be drawn into an unsuccessful challenge.

Improving Your Technique

Do not stand directly in line behind the player you are marking, but at an angle off to one side – preferably in a line between your opponent and the centre of the goal. (The exception is when marking at short corners – in this case you mark from the near post.) This will make you less vulnerable to a quick turn, and give you opportunities to intercept passes on that side, yet allow you to challenge with some momentum for long direct balls played to your opponent. Being positioned slightly away from an opponent gives you more space to counteract flicks and runs, too. You should only challenge when you have a realistic chance of winning the ball, or when the player is about to shoot or pass. The closer your opponent is to goal, the tighter you must mark him.

Exercises

1.   Without using a ball, set up a post and ask a defender to stop an attacker touching it by blocking his path, avoiding body contact. Then give the attacker a ball and ask him to dribble across the pitch in front of the penalty area, seizing any opportunity for a sideways or backward sprint and a shot on goal. Do not do this exercise for too long as it is tiring and can be dispiriting.
2.   In a 25yd (23m) square, set up a three versus three possession game in which players are paired to mark each other and no tackling is allowed. The emphasis is on positioning and intercepting.
3.   Use a small pitch with four attackers versus three defenders marking man for man with the spare attacker allowed only to receive the ball from a back pass. Again, the emphasis is on positioning to avoid through-passes.

Fig 52   Gary Stevens of England seizes the opportunity of a moment's loss of control by Dutchman Ruud Gullit to gain possession.

Intercepting

The Basics

Gathering the ball as it travels between players is the most efficient way of regaining possession, and it usually means you have some space in which to do something with the ball. Intercepting is all about being aware of where players are, judging where the ball can be played, and getting into position to take it without jeopardizing your team if you miss.

Improving Your Technique

After gaining familiarity with patterns of play and building your skills of anticipation, speed off the mark and ball control are the requirements for interceptions. Be positive and act quickly.

In defence, you need to be able to redirect the ball with some accuracy to avoid putting your team-mates in an even more dangerous position by deflecting the ball to another attacker. The aim is to meet the ball full-on, with the meat of the foot or the head, either as a straight clearance or as a controlling move.

In attack, while good ball control will help you capitalize on opportunities from interceptions, any contact with the ball which changes its line of flight can only help your team by forcing the opposition to adjust and possibly regroup. The accent is on speed of thought and movement – and you can afford to take risks and throw yourself towards the ball.

Exercises

1. One player is positioned on each side of the six-yard area, and others on the edge of the penalty box. Shots are fired in towards the goal, and the defenders take turns to move in and control or deflect the ball. The presence of the goal gives a better motivation to reach the ball.
2. Set up two against one in a 20yd (18m) square. Every time the defender gets a touch on the ball, he becomes an attacker and the passer has to try to intercept.

Figs 53 (a)–(d)   Intercepting.

Fig 53 (a)   Marking your opponent at an angle brings opportunities to intercept passes to him. Here the defender is well positioned and alert.

Fig 53 (b)   The defender is ready to move as soon as the pass is struck.

Fig 53 (c)   The defender makes a short sprint past his man.

Fig 53 (d)   This enables him to gather the ball and break up the attack.

Fig 54   Des Walker of England combines ability in the air with speed and
superb tackling skill. The timing of his challenge is usually faultless.

The Intercept Tackle

The Basics

This is a simple piece of opportunism that
can be used when you spot that your
opponent has momentarily lost control.
You poke a toe or foot out to deflect the
ball past him and into a space where you
can collect it.

Improving Your Technique

This is all about timing – knowing when to
strike, and just as importantly, when to
hold back and wait. Your opponent will be
expecting some sort of attack – indeed he
will be hoping to use the moment you
commit yourself in order to make his own
move. Provided he is not taking the ball
into a threatening position, take a little time
so that he will become anxious.

Exercise

Use chalk or rope to make a straight line.
A player dribbles the ball down one side
of it, while a defender moves parallel to
him and aims to deflect the ball without
allowing his whole body to cross the line.

The Block Tackle

The Basics

This is the tackle that is usually employed on '50/50' balls – in other words, when both players have an equal chance of reaching the ball. It is also the most solid form of challenge against a player who is in possession.

Make firm contact with the ball, planting your foot in front of it and pushing through it, with all your body-weight behind the move.

Improving Your Technique

Position your body above the ball as you make contact – a leg or foot left hanging in the way will get injured. Wait for the moment when you feel your opponent has least control of the ball – this is often just before he is about to make contact to dribble or pass. Do not lean back: put your weight on to the attacking leg and go for the block. Aim for the middle of the ball – going too high risks letting the ball slip under, and contact too low gives the opponent a chance to knock the ball on. It is perfectly legal to lean in with your shoulder as an additional block, but of course you must always aim for the ball and not the player. On high challenges, twist the foot as you challenge, as this will bring the ball down.

Exercises

1. Set up a series of drop ball exercises in which a third party drops the ball between two players who challenge for it as it reaches the ground.
2. Put players 2yd (2m) apart with the ball between them. They can challenge for the ball on a given signal. See how many tackles they can win. This will help them

Fig 55 (a)   Get all your weight behind your challenge for the block tackle.

Fig 55 (b)   Power and determination will win the ball.

Fig 55 (c)   This will force it over the opponent's boot.

Figs 55 (a)–(c)   The block tackle.

(a)

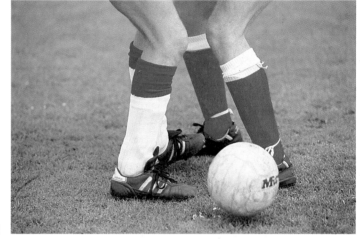
(b)

(c)

Figs 56 (a)–(d)   Tackling a dribbler.

Fig 56 (a)   Jostling your opponent, staying close to him and alert to where the ball is, provides opportunities to tackle the dribbler. Here the player in possession is under pressure.

Fig 56 (b)   He has no time to turn.

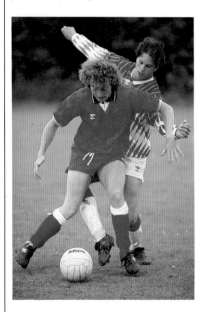

Fig 56 (c)   The defender jostles.

Fig 56 (d)   The defender then gets a toe through the gap to push the ball away.

realize the importance of staying within tackling distance of a player who is in possession, so that they can attack if he loses control of the ball even for a moment.

3.   Use three players, one to set up 50/50 balls for the other two. Progress to a three-a-side game in which players must beat an opponent before passing. This will set up lots of dribbles and tackles.

The Slide Tackle

The Basics

Watch the ball and time your move to meet it, not the man in possession. Bend your supporting leg and slide on the knee and calf of this leg as you put all your weight behind the other foot which blocks and deflects the ball.

Improving Your Technique

The slide tackle commits you totally: if you

Fig 57   The slide tackler tracks his target from behind until he spots his opportunity.

Figs 58 (a)–(c) The slide tackle.

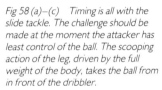

Fig 58 (a)–(c) Timing is all with the slide tackle. The challenge should be made at the moment the attacker has least control of the ball. The scooping action of the leg, driven by the full weight of the body, takes the ball from in front of the dribbler.

(b)

(c)

> **KEY POINT: PITFALLS**
>
> The slide tackle is a weapon in the defensive armoury that can cause injury to its practitioner or victim if it goes wrong.

miss, or are evaded by the attacker, you are out of the game at what could be a crucial few seconds. Use the slide to make up distance you could not make in other ways. Ensure that you will be able to meet the ball from your angle of approach – this usually means attacking from the side, although if your timing is good you may be able to make the move from behind the player in possession. Use the arm and elbow on the attacking side for support as you hit the ground.

Exercises

1. Put a cone 15yd (14m) from two players who stand at right angles to each other, and get them to race to touch it first. The slide is the most efficient way of covering the last few yards. The cone can be replaced by a ball, and after a while you can allow one player to dribble the ball to a point where the defender tries a slide tackle.
2. Send a player off in a straight line with the ball, and when he has travelled 5yd (4.5m), set a defender after him, who has been briefed to execute a legal slide tackle from behind, hooking the ball away with the attacking foot.

> **STAR TIP**
>
> I make sure that my foot is wrapped right around the ball, which enables me to control it. The winger then usually falls over my leg, and this allows me not only to complete the tackle, but also to carry the ball forward myself.
>
> Tony Dorigo [on the attacking merits of the slide tackle]
> *Inside Football*, 14, 1990.

CHAPTER 9

SHOOTING

Every soccer player loves watching the net bulge as he scores a goal, and every soccer player knows that scoring usually looks a good deal easier than it is. Many great scorers were really acting on instinct for many of their goals, and confidence plays a large part in the ability to beat the goalkeeper. However, there are things that can be taught to improve shooting skills.

The first key point is that you should be so familiar with where the goal is in relation to your position that you barely need to look up before making your shot.

KEY POINT: PITFALLS

The common tendency is to end up plugging balls into the middle of the goal, so try to select a target spot to aim at – the stantions are ideal as they are just within the sides of the goal, a vulnerable spot from the goalkeeper's point of view.

The often-quoted golden rule of 'force the goalkeeper to make the save' (in other words, always be on target) conceals the negative thought that he will be able to make a save. Try instead to think 'I am going to beat the goalkeeper'. How do you do that? Start by giving priority to low shots. They present a greater problem for the goalkeeper than shots above the ground, which the human body is better equipped to reach. Never rely on power alone – the cannonball shot will be deflected by even the slightest contact of a desperate hand, but the carefully placed shot will be nestling in the corner of the net while the goalkeeper is still moving across his goal.

There are six ways in which you will beat the goalkeeper: with a powerful drive; a swerving shot (inside or round the goalkeeper); a chip; a volley; a snapshot; or a header. Some of these techniques have already been described in Chapter 5.

Second-Touch Shooting

Second-touch shooting is the way most players start to practice goal scoring, as it gives them control over the placement of the ball and time to choose the shot. Obviously this category also includes shots made after dribbles of any length.

The Basics

Control the ball with one touch. Place your supporting foot firmly and close to the ball, position your head and body so they are over the ball, using your arms for balance, and then strike.

Improving Your Technique

The second-touch shot gives you a fine opportunity to set the best position from which to shoot. This is at a slight angle to the goal, opening it up more than a position directly in front of the goal. Use those moments provided by your first touch to check on the goalkeeper's position. Has he left a gap? If yes, then aim for it. Keep the ball low (unless the goalkeeper is so far out from his line you can chip him). Strike the ball through the middle of its top half, with all the drive coming down from the knee.

Although accuracy is the top priority, power is also important and you should hit the ball so hard your follow-through lifts you off the ground.

Fig 59 If a shot has been hit with power, the whole body will be lifted by the momentum of the kick.

RULES CHECK

A goal is scored if the whole of the ball completely crosses the line. Always follow shots up and if you are in doubt about whether your shot has crossed the line, belt it into the net.

Exercises

1. Test your accuracy on a wall with circles marked on it, or on a goal with track suits hanging from the bar. Do you have the confidence to call 'top right' and hit your target?
2. Change the pace of your two touches.

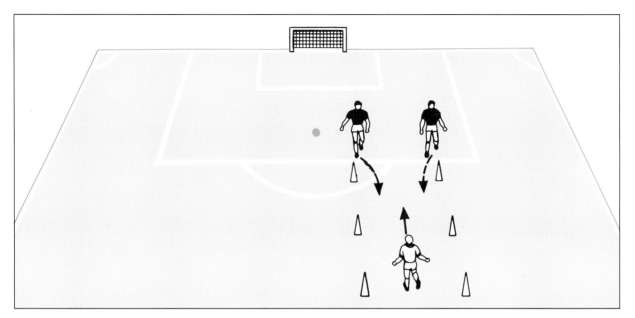

Fig 60   The corridor shooting exercise.

Push the first one ahead and run on to it, and next time use the initial touch just to control the ball and position it for the shot. Do not get into bad habits by always needing a couple of seconds to summon up the shot. Try calling 'one, two' for each touch, and listen to how close those calls can get to each other.

3.   Make a corridor 15yd (14m) wide, running up to the penalty spot. Set an attacker down it with the ball, and allow two defenders to challenge him from the penalty spot. He has to get as near as possible and shoot. Move the corridor around the box so as to avoid too much practice with the players running directly towards the goal face.

First-Touch Shooting

Other factors come into play here: where is the ball coming from; at what height, angle and pace will it reach you; and can you improve on this? Striking a moving ball has more margin for error than hitting a dead ball, but you benefit from carrying the ball's existing momentum into your shot.

The Basics

How you will strike the ball is determined in part by whether it is moving towards or away from you. In the former case, get your supporting foot into position early and allow the ball to approach you (assuming no one can intercept it – in this case you should move towards the ball). Drive right through the centre of the ball with your toes clenched on impact. If the ball is moving away from you, position your supporting foot ahead of it and strike the ball with your toes pointed.

Improving Your Technique

The tendency with balls moving towards the kicker is that he will get underneath them. You should therefore concentrate on placing your supporting foot correctly, keeping your head steady and over the ball on impact, and on striking the ball through its middle line.

If the ball is approaching from a wing, especially the byline, the best shot is probably towards the corner of the goal on the side the ball came from – in other

Fig 61   As the ball falls for the half-volley, the player has the luxury of a deep back-lift of his striking leg to get plenty of power into the well-timed strike as the ball reaches the ground.

Figs 62 (a)–(c)   First-touch shooting.

Fig 62 (a)   As the cross comes over from the right, the goalkeeper tracks across his goal while the attacker moves towards the line of flight.

Fig 62 (b)   The striker can adjust his stride while the goalkeeper's weight is still moving to his right.

Fig 62 (c)   The ball is struck cleanly back towards the right-hand post, past the wrong-footed goalkeeper.

words, back in the same direction. This is because the goalkeeper is likely to be moving in the opposite direction, tracking the ball across. On other occasions, it is generally best to shoot across the goalkeeper towards the far side, as it is harder for a goalkeeper to cover the far post than the near post.

The great benefit of a ball moving from you is that you have the option to strike it on either side, or the middle, so you can be very accurate in your shot placement. You also probably have a little more time than with a cross coming from one side. The drawback is that the ball is escaping from you so you need to be decisive in how you strike it. The worst thing you can do is fail to make any contact at all – many a goal has been scored from a desperately lunging toe-poke at the last second!

Exercises

1.   Always carry out shooting exercises against an enthusiastic goalkeeper, not a reluctant substitute – you will gain no benefit learning how to beat stand-ins.
    Get wingers to cross from either side and make runs that allow you to reach the ball early, but be fully aware of where the goal is and how you are going to shoot.
2.   Use a wall for intensive shooting and controlling practice – mark targets and make sure you use both feet. Shooting against a wall is a great time to experiment with different ways of striking the ball for pace, curve, and so on.
3.   Long, thin practice areas with a goal at one end are ideal for practising how to meet angled through-balls. When you are proficient at timing your run and shot, add a defender to apply some realistic match pressure.

KEY POINT

The shot that gives goalkeepers most trouble is one which bounces just in front of them: the ball will be rising and may change direction slightly through spin or a bump on the ground. So if you can, aim to hit your shots to bounce just beyond the six-yard box line.

The Full Volley

A very high percentage of shooting opportunities come in the form of balls dropping in or around the penalty area. Volleying for goal is an advanced technique that many players, particularly midfielders (who patrol outside the box waiting for stray headers) could use more often.

The Basics

Place your supporting foot next to the spot where the falling ball will bounce, raise the other knee and strike through the ball. Timing is all!

Improving Your Technique

Spread your arms for better balance. Some players prefer to move into the volley by springing up and playing the ball in mid-air. This uses the whole of the body

Fig 63   Balance is the key for the side-on volley.

to drive the shot, but calls for the perfect timing of both jump and strike. Striking with the instep allows you to apply some top-spin to dip the ball under the bar.

To volley bouncing balls coming from one side, do not try to get over the ball, but instead compensate for the height your foot must reach by leaning away from the ball. This will give you balance and will allow you to get your body-weight behind the shot. Spread your arms wide, strike the ball with a sweeping action, and maintain a powerful follow-through. For a particularly high bouncing ball, leap up and strike the ball from mid-air, at the peak of your jump. This move contains an element of surprise which can help to beat goalkeepers.

Exercises

1.   A wall marked with targets, or a goal with objects placed on the line or hung from the bar adds a bit of fun to the necessarily repetitive exercise of moving from the edge of the penalty area to volley in crosses from either side.
2.   Get a player on the edge of the penalty box to throw balls towards the penalty spot for attackers to volley home. After a while, add a defender starting 5yd (4.5m) behind the attacker to put him under pressure.

The Half-Volley

The Basics

The half-volley is used to strike a falling ball just as it is about to hit the ground, or just after its first bounce. Get into position early with the supporting foot firmly in place, and strike through the middle of the ball with the toes pointed.

Improving Your Technique

This is really a matter of improving your timing so that you can strike the ball sweetly every time. Balance is particularly important too, as any lack of poise and steadiness as you strike the ball will be

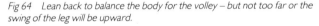

Fig 64   Lean back to balance the body for the volley – but not too far or the swing of the leg will be upward.

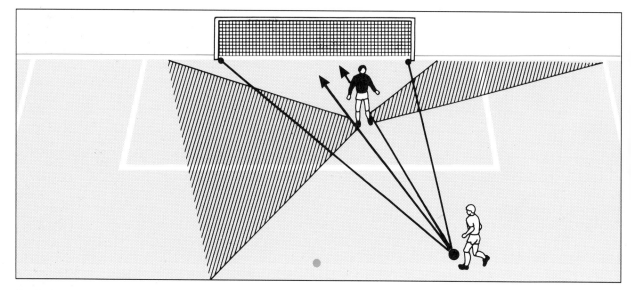

Fig 65   Shots hit across the goalkeeper which he succeeds in parrying are more likely to set up chances for colleagues than those hit to the near post.

magnified into shots that career wildly off course.

Exercises

1   The centre circle is an excellent place to play half-volley tennis without a net. With 6–9 players per team, positioned either side of the centre-line, play a game in which each team defends its half-circle by returning the ball on the volley or half-volley into the other team's area. Play starts with a kick from outside the back of the circle. Second bounces and shots outside the circle are those which score the points.

2.   A wall is a good standby for half-volley practice, as it allows constant repetition of this difficult movement.

The Overhead Kick

Apart from being a spectacular way to strike the ball, the overhead kick has the added benefits of surprise and power. It can be used on any high ball, especially on the bounce, when trajectory and pace are easier to judge.

Fig 66   For the scissor kick, throw the arms back for balance and landing support.

The Basics

Throw your legs up and at the ball, keep your toes pointed, and strike the ball at its centre with the whole weight of your body behind the shot.

Improving Your Technique

The higher you make contact with the ball, the lower its flight will be, so you have to learn to really launch yourself into the kick. You have to be aware of other players around you, as if you make contact with them you will at best be penalized for dangerous play, and at worst, you could inflict a serious injury. In training use a mattress to fall on.

Determining the ball direction from the kick with any accuracy is very difficult, as in addition to the angle at which to strike the ball, and its momentum, you have the added element of your twisted body as it reaches the ball. The element of surprise compensates for this lack of accuracy.

Once you are adept at performing the kick, it can be useful in defensive situations and in switching the direction of play. In these cases, it is often more of a hook than a full scissor kick.

Exercises

1.   Suspend a ball in a net and practise the kick standing up, leaping from the foot that will strike the ball and landing on the other foot. Raise the suspended ball to shoulder height and work on your technique.
2.   Put three players in a line 12yd (11m) apart. The central player has to pass the ball with an overhead kick, and then switches places with the player he passed to.

Fig 67   *The overhead kick requires the legs to be launched into the air, with the body positioned in line with the shot.*

3.   Set up three suppliers to loft balls in for an attacker who must make overhead kicks into goal.

Shooting on the Turn

The Basics

Striking a ball which is coming to you at an angle forces you into a full- or half-turn, driving across the path of the ball. Keep balanced as you move towards the ball, placing your supporting leg in line with the ball. Following a strong back-lift strike across the ball with the instep, keep your head and knee over the ball.

Improving Your Technique

There is a tendency to scoop these shots, and sometimes to wait for the ball to arrive – this invites an interception. You should be able to redirect the pace on the ball into your shot, adding some side-spin or lift at the same time. Remember also the advice on directing your shot towards the part of the goal nearest where the pass

came from so that you can 'wrong foot' the goalkeeper.

Exercise

Stand an attacker near the penalty spot with his back to goal. Have wingers on both sides, and get them to cross and call at the same time, so that the striker has to turn, locate the cross and hit it.

The Snapshot

The snapshot is hit first time, but unlike 'one-touch shooting' described previously, it is an instant, reflex action rather than a considered move.

The Basics

A snapshot is a reaction move, where the ball is struck with little or no back-lift, usually in crowded, fast moving situations.

Improving Your Technique

An ability to strike the ball accurately at pace from any angle is obviously required. The rest of the skill consists of awareness and quick reflexes, both of which come with experience. All great strikers have the knack of recognizing opportunities and greedily seizing them. In the end, it comes down to confidence: if you are scared to miss, you will never attempt a snapshot. If you believe in your ability to score goals, you will consider a shot before any other move with the ball.

Exercises

1. Place an attacker just in front of the penalty spot, and two defenders on the six-yard line, the goalkeeper behind them. Using two crossers on both sides of the

Fig 68   Holland's Marco van Basten has excellent turning skills and a powerful, accurate shot.

box, have balls fired into the danger area. The resulting confusing series of rebounds and half-clearances (the crosses should be no more than two seconds apart) should give the striker a series of half-chances with which to try to score. He will also feel as if he has been inside a pinball machine, so keep each player's session at this practice short but intense.

2. Another excellent exercise uses the good, old brick wall again. Test how many times a player can hit the wall in one minute, standing 5yd (4.5m) from the wall and hitting each rebound as hard as possible. By adding some cones or an object you can produce random deflections, resulting in a particularly realistic practice.

CHAPTER 10

GOALKEEPING

Goalkeeping is the hardest job on the soccer pitch. If players in other positions have an off-day, they just fade from the memory, and even the best teams have weak links in the outfield – but they never have sub-standard goalkeepers.

A bad performance by the goalkeeper usually shows up on the score sheet. Yet quite often very few goals are actually his fault – he can often point an accusing finger at his defence. Goalkeeping is much more than shot-stopping: the goalkeeper has an excellent view of the game as it comes towards him, and when he gets the ball, his choice of distribution is central to the team strategy.

That said, if he cannot collect the ball regularly and safely, no goalkeeper will stay

Fig 70   The fingers should be spread with the opposite thumbs almost touching when collecting the ball.

in the team. Goalkeepers need to be big – tall, with strong hands and a powerful pair of lungs. Good goalkeeping starts with the

stance with feet shoulder-width apart, weight on the soles of the feet, head steady and eyes alert. The best goalkeepers have an aura of authority – the penalty area is their territory, and they dictate how threats to it are handled, either by themselves or by their defenders.

Receiving Balls along the Ground

The Basics

There are two methods of receiving balls along the ground: the stoop, in which the

Fig 69   Goalkeepers should be alert, maintaining a stance with the legs shoulder-width apart, weight slightly forward, and arms in front.

> ### RULES CHECK
>
> The goalkeeper cannot take more than four steps while holding, bouncing, or throwing and recatching the ball. Once he has released the ball he cannot touch it with his hands before another player has been in contact with it. If this 'four steps' law is broken, an indirect free kick is awarded, and with it the threat of a strike at goal from within the penalty area.

Fig 71   For the stooping receive, the goalkeeper keeps both legs straight together in the line of flight, and scoops the ball up.

Fig 72   The kneeling receive places one knee on the ground as a wider barrier in case the hands miss the ball.

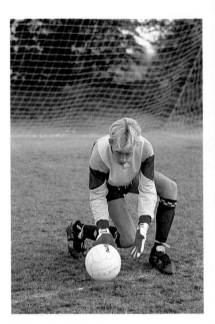

Fig 73   The half-kneeling receive blends the two methods pictured in Figs 71 and 72, combining safety with speed.

legs are kept straight with the feet together and the ball scooped up by the hands; and the kneel, in which the feet and lower body are moved sideways to the line of the ball, and one knee is lowered to the ground to form a barrier in front of which the ball is collected by open hands.

Improving Your Technique

Even if you cannot keep your eyes on the ball as it approaches (perhaps because you are checking on an incoming opponent), the head must be held steady for safe ball collection. The knee of the kneeling leg ought to be level with the opposite heel. Another position, in which the knee is half-lowered to shin level is best for receiving a bouncing ball.

The choice of position for this basic collect is down to the goalkeeper's personal preference. The kneeling stance is generally considered slightly safer.

Exercise

Practise either by kicking a ball at a wall, or asking a colleague to return the ball continuously, perfecting this movement is all about practice and repetition.

Catching at Waist- and Chest-Height

The Basics

Move towards the ball and get your whole body in the line of its flight. Cup the ball into your body which should soften to absorb the impact of the ball.

Improving Your Technique

Keep your eyes on the ball all the way until you have clasped it to your body and there is no risk of it slipping out. Fold your upper body over the ball to prevent it spilling upwards and away. Once you have mastered the basic catch, improvement is down to positioning. Good goalkeepers often do not look spectacular, as they simply seem to shift across a couple of paces and receive the ball. Such nonchalance is down to superb professionalism in being in the right place and anticipating or reacting well.

KIT CHECK

Goalkeepers should always wear padded gloves which offer a good grip of even a greasy and wet ball, and increase the surface area of the hands – thus presenting more of an obstacle for the ball. Gloves should not be over-large, as this lessens control over the ball, and should be elasticated at the wrists to ensure they stay firmly in place throughout the game. When playing in direct sunlight, a peaked cap is a useful aid in countering the blinding effect of looking into the sun as a high ball comes over. The peak should not be so big as to restrict the goalkeeper's field of vision. On hard surfaces, goalkeepers may choose to wear track suit bottoms to lessen the damage caused to legs when falling to the ground.

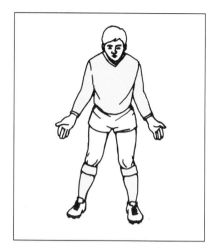

Fig 74 Waist- and chest-height shots should be met by the whole body: feet shoulder-width apart, palms facing out ready to cup the ball into the chest, and eyes fixed on the incoming ball.

Exercise

More repetition I'm afraid – and it might be worth wetting the ball before the session so that it is slightly greasy and slippery as this will show up any lapses very quickly!

Fig 75 Clutch a mid-air ball to the chest and cup the palms round the ball to prevent it slipping out.

Fig 76 Chris Woods of England spreads his body low to block a break by Brazil's athletic striker Careca.

Catching above Head-Height

The Basics

In this case, the hands do not scoop the ball, but are placed behind and to the side of it as the ball is received, with fingers spread. Jump off one leg only, and push out the knee of that leg for extra balance and protection against opponents.

Improving Your Technique

The key is to relax the fingers – rigid, tense hands will allow the ball to rebound away. Relaxed but firm fingers and arms (which should be slightly bent) will welcome the ball and kill its pace. Get the ball down and clasp it to your chest as quickly as possible. You should then bend your knees on landing, and drop on to one shoulder to

take a roll, keeping your head well tucked in at the same time.

Exercise

Position a player about 20yd (18m) away to throw or kick balls at varying heights to you. You can then progress after a while by allowing one player at a time from each side to come forward and challenge for the ball.

Figs 77 (a)–(d)   Catching above head-height.

Fig 77 (a)   The goalkeeper collects a cross. He starts in position towards the back of his goal.

Fig 77 (b)   He then moves towards the highest point where he will be able to reach the ball.

Fig 77 (c)   He collects the ball in both hands.

Fig 77 (d)   Finally he pulls the ball down to his chest and bends his legs to soften the impact of his landing.

Diving

The Basics

The aim is to get your hands on to the ball. Your position should narrow the angle for the shot, your stance should allow you to move easily to either side, and your reflexes should be honed so that you can launch from either leg to spring towards the ball.

Improving Your Technique

This is a tricky blend of alertness and relaxation. A jumpy, tense goalkeeper is light on his feet and seems to glide across the goal. When faced with a shot, his body should relax into the poised, balanced and controlled movement of launching the hands and body at the ball.

The trickiest dive is actually not a dive at all, but a drop on to the ball. A shot blasted low and near a goalkeeper turns his legs into obstructions. These must deliberately be collapsed to make way for the trunk and arms which fall on to the ball.

For full-scale dives, the target should be to dive slightly forward with the hands in front of the body, thus lessening the distance the ball can move away from you.

Always bring your legs in after a dive to lessen the chance of the ball escaping.

Figs 78 (a)–(d)   Diving.

Fig 78 (a)   The goalkeeper moves slightly forwards and into the line of flight.

Fig 78 (b)   The goalkeeper launches himself up off one leg.

Fig 78 (c)   He then clutches the ball.

Fig 78 (d)   The goalkeeper pulls the ball into his body as he lands.

Fig 79   To save low shots close to the body, the goalkeeper must throw his legs away underneath him and drop his body on to the ball.

Fig 80   Attacking a striker who has got clean through, the goalkeeper narrows the angles, then at the right moment throws his legs from underneath to spread himself on the ground and grab the ball.

When diving to the feet (for example, if an opponent is clean through) keep your body low to allow you to swoop down – this also helps to keep your head steady. When diving sideways to present a long block, spread your body wide across the line of the ball's flight – resist the temptation to dive towards the opponent's feet, as this does not narrow the angle.

Exercises

1.   Put chalk lines at right angles to the goal-line about 4yd (4m) apart in the centre of the goal. Players are invited to take shots from between the edge of the area and the penalty spot, and the goalkeeper cannot put his feet down outside those lines. This forces him into a series of dives which, while ignoring the fact that for such shots he would normally be positioned further out, encourage his reflexes and springing technique.
2.   Drop-kick the ball against a wall and collect the rebound as early as possible.
3.   Using a goal without a net, have players taking shots from the front and back.

Shot-Stopping and Deflection

The Basics

The reflex save demands concentration and agility. For deflecting the ball, a decision has to be made early on as to how you will reach it and push it over the bar or the byline.

Improving Your Technique

However experienced the goalkeeper, a mishit or deflected shot often takes an unpredictable line of flight. It is then a question of how the goalkeeper can scramble to get the ball. If his basic stance is good, he will be ready for the movement. The feet should be shoulder-width apart, body-weight on the soles of the feet, head tilted slightly forward and steady, and arms just outside the line of the body.

Exercises

1.   Lie on the ground with the ball on your stomach. Push the ball up with both hands and recapture or deflect it as high as possible at a jump.
2.   Have two players on the six-yard line alternating firing shots towards either post. As soon as you have gathered or have pushed away one shot, the next can be hit.

Collecting Crosses

The Basics

Once you decide to collect a cross, be decisive, and aim to take the ball at the earliest opportunity and maximum height to avoid having to challenge for the ball.

Improving Your Technique

The jumping and holding techniques are

described earlier in this section. However, the arms should be straighter than for collecting high shots – if you have to reach that far up for a shot, it will be going over the bar anyway. The added element is making the choice of which balls you go for and which you leave to your defenders, or accept that an attacker will get there first.

Never move before the ball has been struck, and assess its line, pace and trajectory as quickly as possible, moving as late as possible to actually take the ball. Communication is the key here – if your colleagues know you are coming for the ball, they will allow you unimpeded access and will cover the open goal you leave behind.

If you have to change direction, always turn into the field of play, and never have your back to the action – you will be blind to what is going on.

Exercise

Note: goalkeepers should never practice with an undersized goal, as they will become less familiar with the space they have to defend.

Set a goal up on the half-way line, and get goalkeepers to move up a wing, cross for the other goalkeeper to collect and repeat the move.

Punching the Ball

If the goalkeeper can catch the ball, he should. Punching looks more spectacular but is far riskier and is not usually an efficient form of distribution. However, if he is under severe challenge, or has been forced to move backwards and is therefore insufficiently balanced to catch the ball, he has a choice of deflecting the

Fig 81   The one-fist punch should only be used when under severe pressure. Here the goalkeeper does an excellent job in getting his fist to a ball which the attacker looked sure to reach first.

Fig 82   The two-fist punch should meet the ball head on in its line of flight, and direct it back in the direction from which it came.

ball into touch, or punching it using one or both fists.

The Basics

Decide early on if and how you are going to punch. Ignore the opposition and concentrate on hitting the ball at the earliest opportunity. With the two-fisted punch, aim to get lots of power into the strike. If you can only use one fist, give priority to controlling the direction in which it goes, rather than going for power. Always aim towards the side-lines with your punches.

Improving Your Technique

If you are punching, there will always be an attacker challenging for the ball, so be prepared for some physical contact. You should jump slightly earlier than for a catch, and aim to meet the ball higher, in order to minimize the effectiveness of the challenge. The two-fisted approach is best when attacking along the line of flight. Do not aim for the centre, but towards the bottom of the ball to give height, and aim to make contact with both fists.

For the one-fisted punch, always use your goal-side arm as you will be able to get a better swing, and aim towards the nearest side-line. So at the near post you hit the ball back along its line of flight, and at the far post you punch it out of danger.

Exercises

1.   Suspend a ball high from the bar and practise both kinds of punch without waiting for the swinging ball to stand still.

> **STAR TIP**
>
> To punch well, you must move into a cross with your arm held high and use a quick jab which travels a short distance to impart power in the ball.
>
> Peter Shilton
> Shilton, P. *Goalkeeping in Action*,
> (Stanley Paul, 1988).

2.   Have a fellow goalkeeper hit or throw crosses into the area and challenge an attacker to punch them away. Set up supply lines on both wings to keep up momentum and variety.

Kicking the Ball

You will kick a dead ball when taking goal kicks and some free kicks, and will kick

from the hands at other times. Areas of distribution will be covered in Part 3.

The Basics

To kick a dead ball, read the guidance on passing in Chapter 5 first, and bear in mind that for long kicks you need a long run up and need to drive through the lower part of the ball to gain height. The most common fault with goalkeeper's dead-ball

Fig 83   The drop kick should have power and good direction.

kicks is when they slice the ball because they are watching the target or an opponent instead of keeping their eyes on the ball.

To kick from the hands is unique to goalkeepers and the key is to watch the ball and to relax and swing easily for length in the kick. The weight is transferred from the supporting leg on to the kicking leg for the follow-through.

The drop-kick, when the ball is dropped

from the hands as usual, but not struck until it is about to hit the ground, offers greater distance, but brings risks if conditions are wet or slippery. Read the guidance on the half-volley given in Chapter 9, on shooting.

Improving Your Technique

The difference between the novice and

the professional is one of attitude: beginners get the ball away, but experienced goalkeepers pass to a team-mate, even if he is past the half-way line. This is covered more fully later in the book. The more advanced goalkeeper tends to half-volley because of the speed

RULES CHECK

When facing a penalty, the goalkeeper must be positioned on his line, and cannot move his feet before the ball is struck. If he does, and saves the kick, the penalty will be retaken.

and accuracy it offers, and the greater control in windy conditions.

Exercises

1.   Two goalkeepers can combine kicking practice with collecting high balls, and will enjoy being able to roam the pitch repeating the kick/catch pattern. If no colleague is available, it is back to the good old (and high) wall!
2.   Get goalkeepers to drop-kick to each other, the receiver being punished for any fumble or drop by having to move back 10yd (9m) before he makes his kick. See who can force his opponent down the pitch.

Throwing the Ball

There are three ways of distributing the ball straight from the hands: rolling the ball; throwing from the shoulder; and the over-arm throw. All are generally more accurate than kicking, and a strategically-placed throw can quickly turn defence into attack.

The Basics

The rolled ball is held in the palm while one foot is placed well ahead, coming to a kneeling position as the ball is released level with the front foot and sent away along the ground.

Fig 84   *The kick from the hands is more lofted and a less accurate form of distribution.*

Figs 85 (a)–(c)   Types of throw.

Fig 85 (a)   Rolling the ball is the most accurate method a goalkeeper has of releasing the ball.

Fig 85 (b)   The straight-arm throw should produce a low, fast pass, but the goalkeeper must stay well-balanced as he releases the ball.

Fig 85 (c)   The over-arm throw offers greater distance and can be used to loft the ball over loitering opponents.

The throw from the shoulder is really a push from the palm, the arm beginning behind the shoulder and being extended rapidly in front. The body is kept sideways to the line of flight.

The grip for the over-arm throw is more of a cupping shape using the whole hand – the arm is arced up over the body and the ball is released at the highest point.

Improving Your Technique

Be prepared to take a few paces to gather momentum for the move. For both throws, shift the body-weight from the back to the front foot as you release the ball, to use it as an engine for the push. Take care not to release the ball early as this sends the ball skywards and can twist and damage the hand. Try to throw flat from the shoulder for greater accuracy.

Exercises

1.   Using half the pitch with goals at each end, set teams of two or four goalkeepers the task of retaining possession just by throwing and catching (one bounce allowed) and aiming to score goals. As a variation, drop-kicks can be added.

Positioning

Although positioning is arguably the most important element in a goalkeeper's game, it is also the hardest to learn, and it has been left to the end of this chapter because players will really appreciate the value of good positioning once they

discover how difficult it is to reach the same ball from different places in the goal. The best shot in the world is easy to save if you happen to be standing in its path.

The Basics

The goalkeeper should try to be in a position which restricts the target at which an attacker can aim. This involves leaving the goal-line and moving towards the

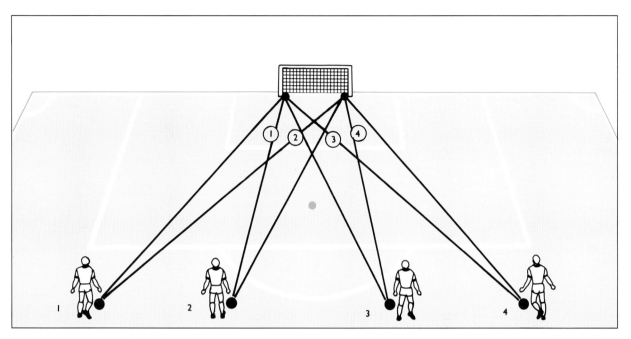

Fig 86   Four attacking positions and the appropriate placing for the goalkeeper. Moving towards the attacker will narrow his potential shooting angles.

threat in a way which narrows the potential scoring space, also called the angles of opportunity.

Improving Your Technique

Obviously it is important to be near enough the ball to threaten it, and not too far from the goal to allow the ball to be lobbed over you. However, more complex decisions have to be made if, say the ball is on the flank and may be crossed over. Here you need to be positioned towards the far side of the goal to give you space in which to attack a cross. If the player moves from the flank to threaten the goal, the goalkeeper must move across to narrow the angle.

The key in all this is a blend of judgement and balance. The ability to assess how far you should move from the goal, and which parts of it are most vulnerable, can really only come with experience. However, the best position is ruined if you cannot maintain it and topple as the forward advances. The goalkeeper should be able to stop his run outwards at any point and remain poised. He must try to make himself as big as possible by standing up with arms spread, presenting the most difficult physical block to a shot.

Exercises

1.   Stand 6 players spaced apart just outside the penalty area. Get the goalkeeper to position himself as if the player on the right has the ball, then on counts of two, he must adjust his position as if the next player along is in possession.
2.   Once he is happy with his positioning, allow the attackers to interpass a ball, not necessarily to the nearest player. If they feel the goalkeeper has left a gap, they can shoot for goal.
3.   Goalkeepers often have to move sideways like a crab – get them to do this in training instead of sprints.

PART 3
TACTICS

CHAPTER 11

WHAT ARE TACTICS?

Soccer tactics are becoming increasingly sophisticated, and an understanding of them is essential for a good player and for the informed spectator. Tactics are simply the plan and sub-plans to which teams work: from 'get the ball into the opposing penalty area' or 'build moves from the back four', to more detailed instructions such as 'force their left winger infield' and 'keep a man on their key midfield player' For youngsters playing soccer, tactics should not be a major consideration – enjoying the game and developing skills are far more important. But while soccer is a simple game, a match can be the vessel for

a great deal of thought about the game, and how it should be played. So an understanding of soccer tactics helps improve the game for everyone.

Formations and Team Tactics

Team formation is a fascinating element in soccer tactics that requires a good understanding of the game from all the players involved so that changes or adjustments are properly implemented.

The development of the modern game

can be traced through the changing fashions of formations since the 1950s. Early in that decade, 2–3–5 was the standard formation: two full-backs, three centre-halves, and five forwards (two wingers, a tall centre-forward and two inside-forwards who covered a central channel and helped out in midfield).

When Hungary memorably defeated England 6–3 at Wembley in 1953, they used a new system of play. They played with a centre-forward deep in midfield, and highly attack-minded inside-forwards. To an English defence in which the centre-half was drilled to cover the opposing

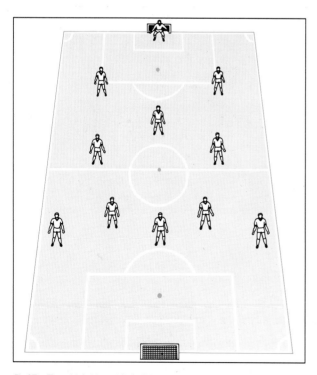

Fig 87   The old-fashioned 2–3–5 formation, in which the inside-forwards were the link between midfield and attack.

Fig 88   The 4–2–4 allows the use of wingers but leaves a sparse midfield pairing in front of the back four.

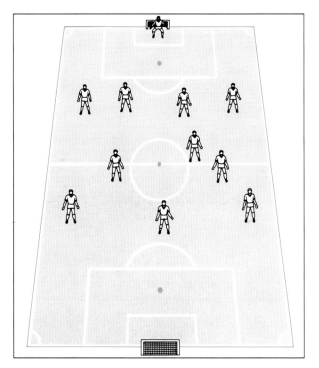

Fig 89   The 4–3–3 involves the use of one winger and offers a more balanced midfield with better covering possibilities.

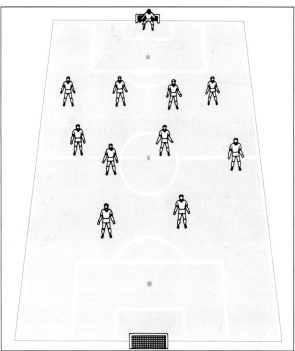

Fig 90   The 4–4–2 packs the midfield which must support the two front runners quickly in attack.

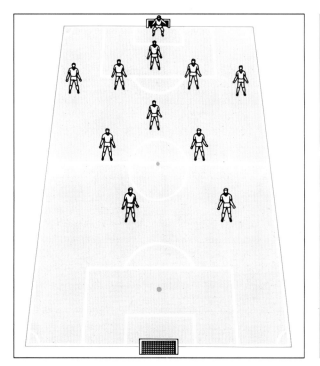

Fig 91   Playing a sweeper behind the back four creates 5–3–2, a highly defensive formation suitable for absorbing pressure and making quick counter-attacks.

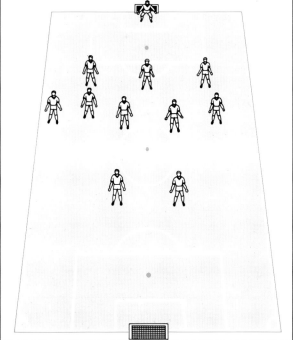

Fig 92   The 3–5–2 involves the use of three centre-backs with the wings covered by full-backs who have a key midfield and overlapping role.

centre-forward, while the centre-halves pivoted around him (so if the left-half was up, the right-half was back), this was totally bemusing. The centre-half was pulled out of position, while the full-backs stayed deep and left the Hungarian inside-forwards Kocsis and Puskas on side and in space.

Further development of new formations was seen in the Brazilian World Cup-winning side of 1958. This spread four defenders across the back, to deny opposing wingers space. The logical progression from this was to have four players forward and two in midfield. Thus was born the 4–2–4 system, quickly refined to 4–3–3 when heavy midfield pressure forced them to pull an attacker back.

These formation changes altered not merely the space players covered, but their role in the match. Teams cut out one winger to gain a player in midfield, and began to encourage attackers to work from deeper positions. Full-backs were now playing wider, with more central support, and were able to move forward and act as wingers at times. The squareness of the back four defence players was countered by the use of a sweeper positioned behind them to cover any breaks in the wall, and in some cases this role was moved just in front of the back four, breaking up attacks before they made an attempt to get through towards the goal.

Most recently, some teams have taken to playing with three central defenders, pushing the full-backs well into midfield and making more use of wingers to stretch the opposing defence – a 3–5–2 formation in attack, working as 5–3–2 or even 5–4–1 in defence.

Fig 93   Good team tactics accommodate players' individual talents with an overall playing pattern which limits opponents' strengths and exploits their weaknesses – this is how goals come about.

CHAPTER 12

DECIDING TEAM TACTICS

The fundamental rule for a coach devizing a playing formation for a team is to use the available resources to their best effect, rather than asking players to change their style of play to your system. The latter is simply a case of the 'tail wagging the dog'. If the team features two superb wingers, use them to pull defences apart, and support them with full-backs behind and attackers making late central runs to receive their crosses. If, on the other hand, you have no natural wingers but have creative midfield players who are able to pick off attackers from long distances, then support those midfield players with strong tackling ball winners, and be prepared to use three strikers down the central area, with the wings left for the full-backs to roam in.

No team is made up of 11 players of equal ability. It makes sense to build the team tactics around the playing styles of those best-equipped players who are likely to be in the team regularly, and who are able to sustain a pattern of play which their colleagues will understand and adapt to. Once the team tactics are agreed, it is important to remind players of them, and to refine them through discussion and experimentation. That said, it is pointless to try to impose a playing style through every minute of the match: the best players are often opportunists who recognize a chance to do something

different and should be encouraged to try it – after all, unpredictability is the best weapon in any sport.

There are several basic tactical ploys of which every team should have some understanding: applying pressure, absorbing pressure, changing tempo, and balance.

Applying Pressure

Pressure can win games. You may have the slower, less skilful players, but if they are constantly battling, closing down space, challenging opponents who dally on the ball, and moving forward with determination, they can unsettle their superior opponents and defeat them. The whole team should try to apply pressure from the moment possession is lost. After all, the most vulnerable position in which to find yourself is when trying to control the ball on your own goal-line! So attackers should understand that they have an important role in unsettling the opposition.

Some teams build from the back by playing the ball across the back four, perhaps looking for opportunities to stretch the opposing defence and make a long pass over the midfield area. Their defenders are able to linger on the ball and pick the moment to pass – but only if no one is challenging them. Opponents who are given time on the ball usually gain confidence, which encourages them to try something unusual – this could catch out the defence and gain a goal. An attacker can therefore help his defence even if he is only covering space for a pass, or forcing the opposition to keep moving the ball across rather than forward. Three attackers should be able to cover four defenders by forcing them across, and

covering space for any alternative passes. When the moment is right and the defence is under pressure, a midfielder can move up to turn the tactic into a man-on-man marking system.

Timing of challenges is important. Leaping in to tackle at the earliest opportunity is not necessarily the best option, especially in hot conditions. Forwards can be better advised to contain defenders and wait until they are near the half-way line before making a challenge. That way, if they win the ball, they have more space to exploit as the defenders will be out of position.

Exercise

Take ten players and ask one to drop out to set up four forwards against five defenders on a small pitch. Award marks for every touch the forwards get on the ball. After two minutes, bring on the spare man as a substitute and have another two minutes' activity. The aim is to get the forward line to work as a team in order to close down space and prevent the numerically-superior opponents from getting past them.

Even packed defences can be put under pressure by being stretched. This is where the value of off-the-ball runs becomes apparent. Wingers pushing out wide, perhaps supported by full-backs who threaten to move into space inside them, force defenders to spread themselves more thinly across the pitch, leaving gaps to be exploited.

Pressure is increased during attacks if the defence moves up to support the front line. Some coaches aim to have all players except the goalkeeper within one 40yd (37m) band of the pitch – the back defender is therefore always less than a

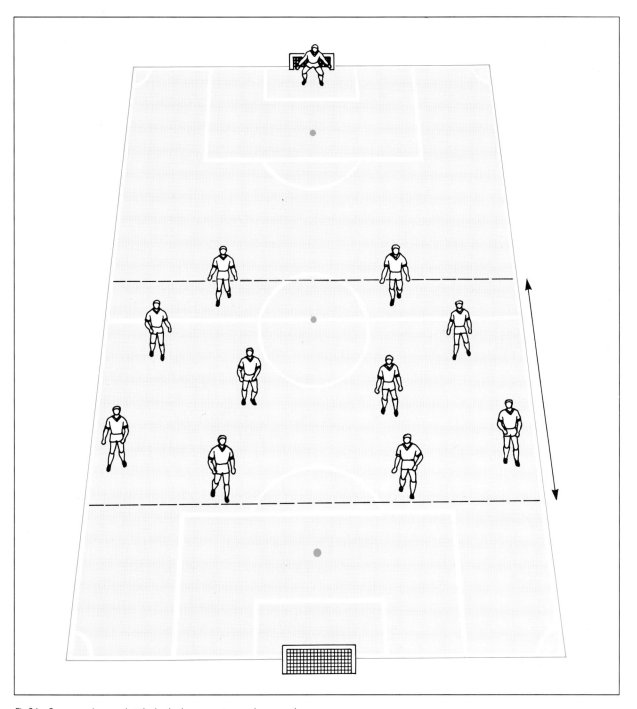

Fig 94 Some coaches say that the back players must never be more than 40yd (37m) behind the attackers. This pressurizes opponents and denies them space in a compressed midfield.

half-pitch length away from the front attacker. This forces the opposition back and limits their passing opportunities if they win the ball.

The idea works for defence, too. Whenever the opposition play the ball backwards, the defence should push up, lessening the space available for an attack. If a forward makes a run behind the defenders into space, leave him: he will be off-side when the ball is put through.

Absorbing Pressure

Some teams have mastered the art of absorbing pressure. They are content to be pinned into the final third of the field, soaking up attacks, and then suddenly breaking with great speed to exploit a weakened opposition defence. Teams can be coached to absorb pressure by being organized – in other words, by understanding the team pattern and the role of each member. Such organization breeds enormous confidence when the team sees it running smoothly.

Tempo

The team that sets the tempo of a match usually wins it. Some teams enjoy fast, frenetic action which unsettles opponents. Others play passes around their half of the field, waiting for chances to make a telling pass and relieving pressure on the team in the meantime – nothing is as demoralizing as realizing that your team has not touched the ball for the last minute. The experienced members of the team should set the appropriate tempo, and constantly communicate it to their colleagues through calls on movement, whether to hold the ball, and so on.

Fig 95   Certain ploys, such as hitting early long balls, or spreading play to the wings, form part of the team strategy. It requires players with good brains for football such as Bryan Robson to implement these plans.

CHAPTER 13

ATTACK

Football matches are only won through attack: defence merely prevents you losing. Even for the born goal scorer to whom the act of hitting the net is instinctive, an understanding of tactical attacking, which is really a way of recognizing and achieving your best option, is invaluable.

Shooting

It may seem odd to start a chapter on attacking tactics with shooting – after all, shooting is often largely an instinctive act. But the aim of any soccer team is to score goals as this is the only way of winning a match, and there are tactical aspects to shooting that help everyone from the experienced striker to the novice centre-back to beat the goalkeeper. Part of that tactical knowledge is an awareness of when not to shoot.

When Not to Shoot

It is pointless shooting if:

1.   You are too far from the goal to have a realistic chance of beating the goalkeeper.
2.   The shooting angle is too tight.
3.   A defender is obviously going to be able to block the shot.
4.   A colleague is in a better position with a clear shooting chance.

Placing the Shot

Accuracy is more important than power in shooting – a goalkeeper can get in the way of a cannonball shot without even seeing it, but the well-placed effort will attack the most vulnerable part of the goal and luck will not keep the ball out.

Fig 96   There is no point shooting from this position – two defenders stand in the line of flight, ready to intercept the shot, and the goalkeeper is unlikely to be threatened from this distance as he is under no pressure.

The most vulnerable part of the goal is either the area that has been left unguarded, probably by a positional error (for example, if the goalkeeper has moved too far across, his near post should be threatened, and if he is too far from his goal a lob will find the net), or the area the goalkeeper is moving away from. For example, a cross from the right will force the goalkeeper to move left across his goal, and a shot back towards the right-hand side of the goal therefore requires him to make a total change in direction if he is to retrieve it.

In other cases, the simple rule when shooting is to strike the ball across the goalkeeper towards the far side of the goal. Shots to the near side allow the goalkeeper to attack the ball, and any deflection is likely to put the ball out of play and out of danger. Going for the far side, however, forces the goalkeeper into attempting a save behind his body, and deflections are more likely to push the ball across the goal or out from it – easy meat for attackers following up.

The Long Shot

Long shots put pressure on goalkeepers who know that if they fail to hold the ball, there are attackers close by who will pick up the rebound. Long shots require power and accuracy and most players prefer to allow the ball to run across them before striking. Long shot opportunities frequently come from clearances from the penalty area, with the added benefit that the goalkeeper is probably unsighted.

Exercise

Have crosses played in and headed out by defenders, to be struck back in by players waiting about 10yd (9m) outside the penalty area.

Creating Space

Attackers need to find, or make space at many times. This is most obvious if they are in possession near the goal and want to shoot, but is needed at many other times in the final third of the pitch when they are likely to be closely marked. The overall aim here is not to attack the goal: the target is the space between defenders and the goalkeeper, for this is the area in which scoring opportunities arise.

None of the tactics discussed here have any value unless your ball control is good enough for you to ensure that you retain possession while making space for a pass or shot. Turning techniques are an excellent way of making space when in

possession, but making space off the ball is just as important.

Making Space as a Team

The simplest tactic for making space is to stretch the opponent's defence. Whether they are playing a zonal or man-for-man system, by having players positioned on each wing, you will force them to deploy resources across the field. That creates gaps in the centre, and in midfield.

Another tactic to make space is for two attackers to switch positions: it forces defenders to choose whether to mark a different, less familiar opponent, or to swap positions themselves, which tends to create empty spaces. Forcing defenders to change their pattern of play usually provides opportunities for sowing confusion in their ranks.

To combat man-for-man marking, players can make switching or cross-over runs. Here they move diagonally across each other's path, using the meeting point to exchange the ball and continue in the same direction, or to change running angles and confuse defenders. All such moves should be made with a burst of acceleration to further distract the defenders. An attacker can legitimately

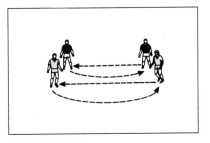

Fig 98 Swapping positions forces markers to either follow (leaving spaces behind them) or switch which man they mark. It sows doubt in the minds of defenders and gives them another problem to deal with.

protect a team-mate in possession by making a parallel run that blocks the path of an intercepting defender. If the attacker is in the space first, he is within the laws of the game to occupy it.

Creating a spare player makes opportunities. Defenders facing two players will try to retreat and simultaneously keep an eye on both of them. But if they are attacked and forced to commit themselves, they can be isolated. The key is to get players to find space in close support positions, not vast distances from the action.

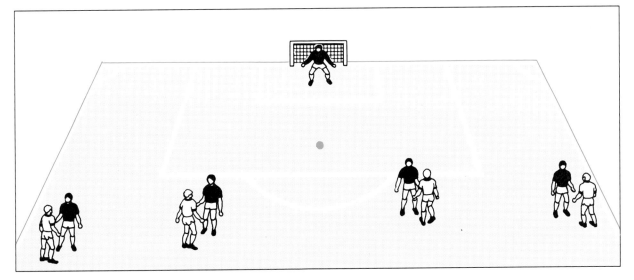

Fig 97 Wingers stretch a defence, creating space for supporting midfielders to exploit.

Exercises

1.   Set up two players against one in a 10yd (9m) square. The spare player has to work hard to make space in such a tight area, and the man in possession must try and make the defender commit himself before passing to his colleague.

2.   Raise the stakes in a slightly larger area with two against two, with attackers being forced to move all the time to make space. Then extend the practice area to 20yd (18m) by 10 yd (9m) and allow them to score goals. This will help them develop the technique of checking back, leaving the marker covering thin air.

3.   Using an area 30yd by 10yd (27m by 9m), with a player at each end, get two players to compete for the ball in the middle. They should then pass to one end, take a return ball and reach the fourth player at the opposite end.

Making Space Individually

Getting away from your marker, particularly behind him, makes the defender uncomfortable as he cannot watch you and the ball at the same time. The prime requirement here is speed off the mark – the ability simply to leave your marker behind and get into space to receive the ball.

Exercise

One exercise for building speed off the mark is to set up timed sprints and shuttle runs and to keep a chart of each player's improvements over the weeks. At the same time, count how many strides a player needs to cover, say 20yd (18m). If he can lengthen his stride but keep his legs

moving at the same rate, his overall speed will increase.

There are more subtle ways of escaping your marker, though. If the opposition is playing a zonal defence system, in which players mark areas of the pitch, attackers can repeatedly move between adjacent zones, forcing defenders to keep handing over to a colleague or be drawn across, leaving a gap for another attacker to exploit.

If you watch schoolboy soccer players, you will see them running in straight lines towards the goal. Adult teams should have attackers who move diagonally, taking defenders across the pitch with them, checking back for the ball or to make space, or running on a curve that allows them to maintain momentum for a run towards goal without straying off-side.

Exercise

Get pairs of players to shadow each other around the pitch, one trying to lose the other by changing direction and pace at will.

Making Space to Collect a Pass

Space can also be created by the way in which you collect a pass. A straight call for the ball to be played to your feet will alert defenders to the threat. Feinting to move one way, then dodging back or across to another position, gives your team-mates the opportunity to play the ball into the space you are going to occupy. You can also use the ploy of moving towards the passer, then suddenly turning and sprinting back from where you came, leaving a defender stranded between the ball and the striker. The tighter a defender is marking his man, the easier it is to escape him with these unpredictable and rapid movements.

Attackers tend to turn away from defenders when trying to escape them. In fact, there is much merit in turning into them and sprinting past before they have time to react. This forces them into trying a tighter turn to catch up, which makes it harder for them to maintain their balance.

Blind-side running allows you to create

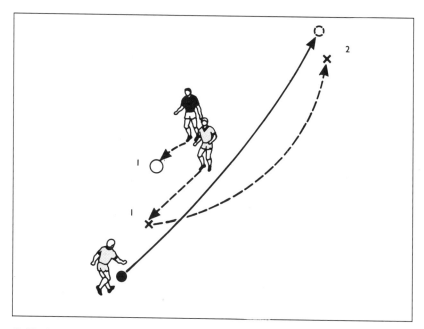

Fig 99   *Making space for a pass is never easy, but a decoy run towards the ball, followed by a quick turn and a curving run into the path of the pass can put defenders in trouble.*

Figs 100 (a)–(f)   The crossover run.

Fig 100 (a)   Crossover runs confuse defenders and should be practised regularly to maintain the understanding between attackers. Both players set off on curving runs towards each other.

Fig 100 (b)   They are tracked by their markers.

Fig 100 (c) and (d)   They make a dummy and change of direction.

Fig 100 (d).

Fig 100 (e)   This throws the defender.

Fig 100 (f)   There is now space to receive the pass.

Fig 101   Blind-side runs require good timing and can get players into a surprising amount of space.

space by arriving in areas where defenders are not expecting you. The key is to plan your move, time your run to meet the ball behind defenders, and to run in a curve taking you out of the defender's line of vision. This takes practice and it can be demoralizing if once you make the move, your team-mates fail to get the ball to you. However, as a decoy run in which you take a defender with you it can be as valuable as a through-ball, creating gaps in the defence for other players to exploit. So discuss the move, and practice plays in which an attacker makes a decoy run away from the ball or dummies it to allow it to travel into the space you are heading for. Use the ideas behind your set-piece ploys at other times in the game if you can see opportunities.

Exercises

1.   Stand two players 30yd (27m) apart and get them to chip over a defender who is positioned between them. The defender can then attack the player in possession. Start the exercise with the receiver not being allowed to move, forcing the player with the ball to make enough space to strike the pass.

2.   To practise the decoy run with the pass into space, place players 15yd (14m) apart. Get one player to sprint diagonally across the other, who then feints to pass and dribbles with the ball for a few yards before passing. Now bring in a defender, and have the ball played to the man

marked. He lays it off for the other player, turns and sprints, leaving the defender with the task of attacking the new player while covering the return pass.

3.   Now in a 25yd by 15yd (23m by 14m) area, practise the blind-side run. The ball is with a marked player and the other player goes on to the blind side while calling for the ball. The defender has to peel off to cover the space, or allow the ball to be passed. Set up a two versus two game in which the aim of every move is to gain space or act as a decoy.

Through-Balls

There are two characteristics to a top-quality pass – it should enable the receiver to do something with the ball first time, and will probably be played between two opponents, taking both of them out of the game. The true through-pass achieves both these aims.

Through-passes punted hopefully into space are pointless unless someone on your team can collect them: the through-pass is a co-ordinated move by at least two players, with others probably involved in making space for the pass. A retreating defence in particular fears being run at and having balls played through at pace.

Fig 102   The through-pass should cut defenders out of the game, and is usually played through the gap between them.

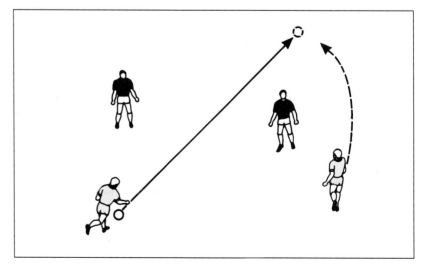

Figs 103 (a)–(c)   The through-ball.

Fig 103 (a)   The through-ball is a combination of passing and running skill by two players. The ball is played between two defenders.

Fig 103 (b)   They beat the marker of the runner.

Fig 103 (c)   The marker has moved on the blind side and receives the pass in a position to threaten the goal.

If the defence are using sweepers, the through-pass becomes a difficult task in which the strike and the run have to be synchronized. Moves like this have to become habit: as a player receives the ball, at least one colleague should start his diagonal run, aiming for the space behind defenders, and the pass should be a calculated strike into that space, so that only the on-running attacker can reach it.

Exercises

1.   Getting the weight of the pass right is important. Using three players in an area 25yd (23m) square, one plays a pass which will reach the other end of the area at the same time as a sprinting player without the latter having to check his stride. This player then controls the ball and plays a similar pass for the waiting third man. Now add a return pass before the long through-ball. Practise the move with the pass being made at an angle, and alongside the player, the latter being trickier to perfect.

2.   Play three versus three in the penalty area, with the defending side forced to use one player as a goalkeeper. The spare opposing player aims to hit through-balls to the marked strikers. This exercise can be converted to a bigger game using half the pitch, and giving the defenders a target man to hit the ball to if they win it. If the target man can reach the centre circle this counts as a goal.

Switching the Direction of Play

This sounds more technical than it actually is. Switching the direction of play often merely means getting the ball into the most dangerous place for the opposition. This will usually be where there is most space. So if there is no cover on one side

Fig 104   (Overleaf) Modern attackers must be prepared to make countless intelligent runs to make space for others or themselves, and they must get into the danger area first to snap up chances. England's Gary Lineker has a tremendous work rate throughout a match.

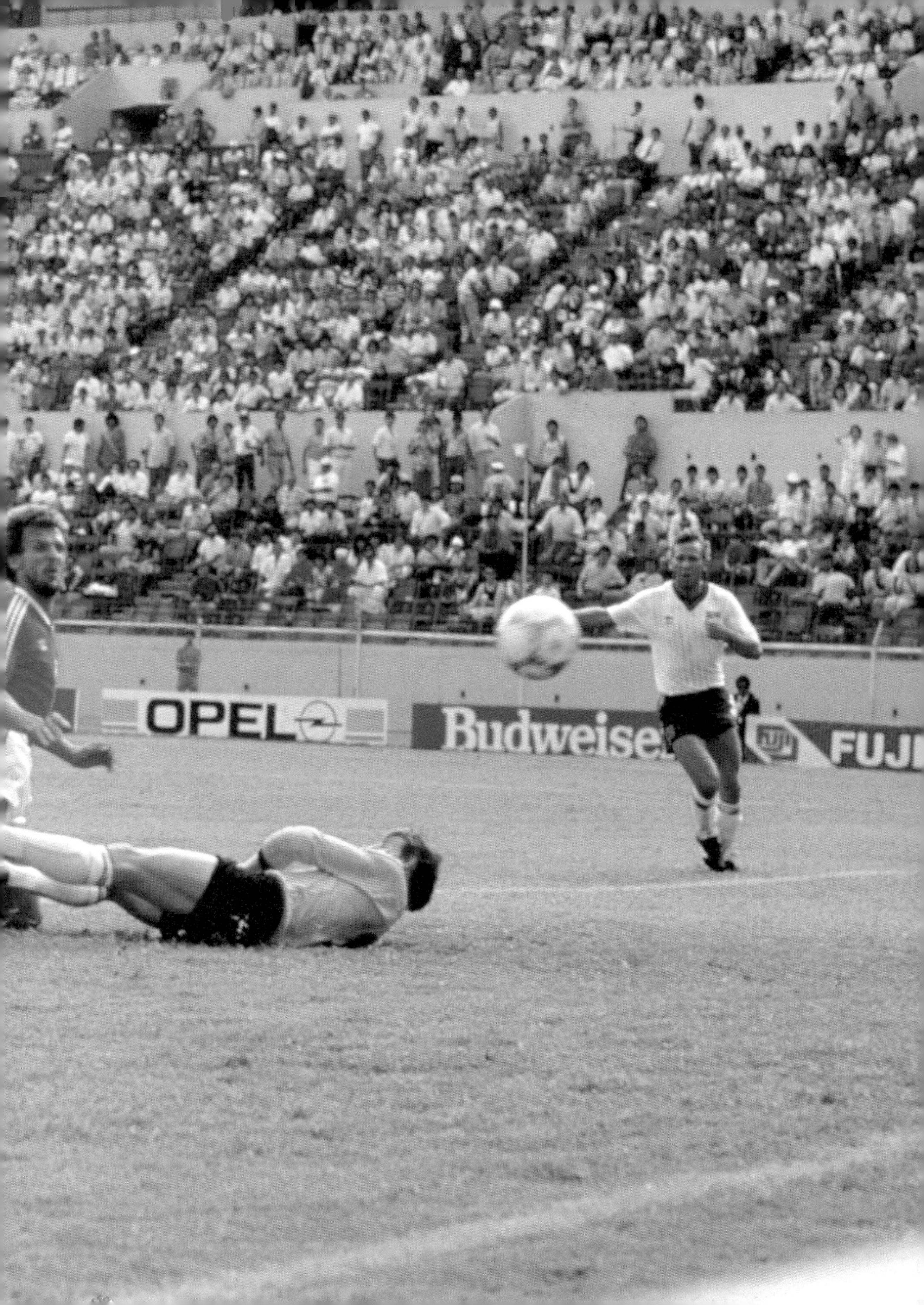

OPEL
Budweiser
FUJI

of the defence, that is where a full-back or winger will be moving towards, and where the ball should be played. This requires good vision, and sufficient familiarity with the principles and pattern of the game to know that if you are facing the sweeper on the left wing, he has left a gap in the centre of the defence – and one of your colleagues should be heading for it.

Laying Off

Centre-forwards are often the focal points of attack, not because they are capable of scoring goals, but because they set up chances for supporting players. They often receive the ball with their back to goal and look to play it into the path of an onrushing team mate. The best place to put the ball is not in line with the run, but at an angle up to 15yd (14m) away. This allows some margin for error in the pass, which is likely to be made under pressure.

The target man should be thinking about his best position throughout the game, even when the opposition is in attack (after all, if his team-mates win the ball, they will be looking to get it to him). He must have excellent close control to be capable of accepting passes hit at any angle, height or pace, controlling the ball, shielding it, and laying it off.

Exercises

1. Play three front and three midfield players against a back four with one midfielder and a goalkeeper. Midfielders play the ball up to a forward who must lay it off for one of them to set up a scoring attempt. The rule is to support the man in possession, and to learn to anticipate play by staying aware of what is happening and what could happen next.

2. Put an attacker just outside the penalty box, with team-mates in the centre circle and an opposing defender and goalkeeper between him and the goal. His colleagues hit balls up to him and the passer moves in for the lay off – although the attacker can use this as a decoy and turn and shoot himself. Now add a second defender in front of the attacker so that he has to

create space to receive the ball in the first place.

Wing Play

Space is most easily found or created on the sides of the pitch – the wings. Wingers, be they attackers or supporting midfield players, have a crucial role in inventive soccer. This is because during a match they have opportunities to attack individually with dribbles, to come inside and shoot, or to make the crosses that central strikers feed on. Once seeming to go out of fashion, the winger's role has recently undergone a major resurgence. However, modern wingers are more than dribblers and crossers – today they are also expected to support the midfield by covering and ball winning to a much greater extent than their predecessors.

Wingers need acute tactical awareness to know when to go inside, when to cross early, and when to wait for more support to arrive. Although chances can be made, particularly for themselves by cutting inside, wingers generally aim to get to the byline to make the cross, because balls coming away from the goal are harder for the goalkeeper to attack, and easier for colleagues to strike. (Defenders recognize this and usually try to push the winger towards the centre of the pitch rather than let him go down the outside.) There are five routes to the byline:

1. Meeting a long through-ball.
2. Dribbling past the full-back.
3. Passing the ball down the line for a central striker to move on to.
4. The overlap.
5. The wall pass.

All of these are covered in Part 2, except the overlap, a technique as useful for attacking full-backs as wingers.

The Overlap

Wingers and full-backs often work in pairs to achieve the overlap. The simplest form of overlap involves a player on the outside sprinting past a marked colleague in

possession, and having the ball delivered into his path. More complicated variations include the player going on a curving run from inside the player in possession, still moving for the ball on the outside, but often taking a defender with him and leaving space which the ball holder can exploit. The overlap remains an invaluable method of committed attack, and therein lies its weakness – if the ball is lost, the player is marooned well away from the action.

Exercise

Practise the move without defenders, starting 20yd (18m) outside the box and to the side. Get the timing of the run and the pass perfected before adding a defender and, eventually, more players in the centre to contest the cross.

Crossing

Crossing is one of the major tests of any player, both in the technique of accurate placement of a ball hit at speed, and the tactical sense of when and where to play the ball.

Timing the Cross

Wingers should be good, fast dribblers, capable of moving the ball along with any part of either foot. If their team-mates can match their pace, an early cross will put maximum pressure on the defence and will be most useful to the attack. If the winger is slower, or if more support is needed, he can go for the byline and pull the ball back for his team-mates, or he may decide, one he has glanced up, that he must hold the ball before crossing. The key here is not to get trapped into trying to hold the ball in a tight spot, such as near the corner flag: the decision to hold should be taken earlier, about level with the outside of the penalty area.

Fig 105 (a)–(f) The overlapping full-back has brought a new dimension to wing play. The key to success is in the timing of the blind side run and the skill of the returner in laying it off.

Figs 105 (a)–(f)   Wing play – the overlap.

Fig 105 (a).

Fig 105 (b).

Fig 105 (c).

Fig 105 (d).

Fig 105 (e).

Fig 105 (f).

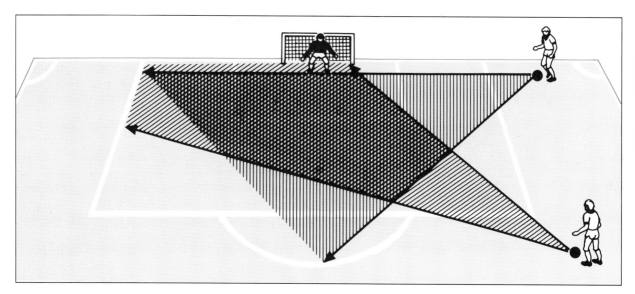

Fig 106 The cross from the byline is harder for goalkeepers to attack because the potential angle is wider and the ball is moving away from them. Crosses from infield positions are more limited and the ball is coming towards the goalkeeper: he will lap them up.

Depth is needed in attack, because if players are in a straight line, the winger is forced into trying to play the ball square. This is most apparent at poor standard games where a hesitation in crossing leaves the attackers stranded ahead of the ball.

Exercise
You need two trios of attackers and three defenders. The centre-forward passes to the winger, who has to beat his man and cross for the two incoming forwards. Then the next wave tries. The choice of winger should be alternated. It may be helpful if the wingers try this exercise whilst playing a defending position, to get a feeling of what it is like facing a winger and what makes the defender feel most uncomfortable.

Fig 107 The main danger area is an oblong patch 10–15yd (9–14m) from the goal. The crosser has three routes to get the ball there: direct (a); then via an intermediate player (b); or over it and back from a wide player (c).

Placing the Cross

The elements that determine placement of the cross are the positions of defenders and attackers, and where space is available. Crosses should always be hit into space ahead of attackers, not played direct to them.

Crosses are best aimed towards the hardest areas to defend – the posts – although the actual target is the edge of the six-yard line level with the post. Whenever possible, they should be angled so that defenders have to travel backwards to challenge – this can create a great deal of space for attackers. Know the options related to the types of cross. The near-post chip gives the attacker the choice of flicking on or shooting, and is best suited to small, quick forwards. The far-post cross should be curling away from the goalkeeper and is best met by taller, powerful players. When the penalty area is crowded, the low driven cross stands a good chance of being deflected by any player, attacker or not, to create an opening.

When playing the ball into the space between defenders and the goalkeeper for a forward, it is best to aim at the near post. This gives the defence less time to attack the ball and less opportunity for the goalkeeper to intercept.

The near-post cross

These should be played to land behind defenders, so are usually better played well back from the byline as otherwise defenders will have had time to take up position while the winger reached the line. That said, the goalkeeper is more likely to be positioned at the back of his goal if the winger has reached the byline, as he will be expecting to attack a deeper cross.

The central cross

A cross hit into the area 5–10yd (4.5–9m) out from the centre of the goal makes a most inviting target for attackers. This area is usually well defended, so attackers should work as a team to make space, perhaps one moving away from the area towards the cross, taking a defender with

him, while a colleague makes a late run into the space. Central crosses should not be lofted in as this gives defenders time to adjust to the threat: rather they should be chipped or side-footed in for speed and accuracy.

The far-post cross

This cross aims to bypass the goalkeeper and be met by an incoming attacker arriving at an angle, so that when he meets the ball he is facing the goal. The closer to the sideline the winger is, the harder it will be to deliver the ball accurately, but the easier it will be to loft the ball over the goalkeeper. If the winger is nearer the penalty box, his cross stands more chance of being intercepted as it will not have sufficient height to beat the goalkeeper. Instead it should be either angled back further to put it out of his range, or hit deeper so that it is likely to be headed back into the goal area rather than struck at goal.

Exercise

On a small 30 by 15yd (27 by 14m) pitch with small goals, set up a three versus three with the defenders forced to use one player as a goalkeeper. This sets up a series of three versus two attacks dependent on a triangle formation being formed with one player ahead, one behind. Build up the game to say ten versus seven players on a full pitch, with no dribbling allowed. This forces players to pass into space for the ball to be crossed.

Set Pieces

Set pieces are the major source of goals in football, accounting for nearly half of the goals scored in the professional game. Clearly, amid the extended improvization that characterizes most of the game, these moments when the whole team knows what is going to happen next, and what their part is in turning the move into a goal – while the opponents are merely aware that something is in the pipeline – are crucial to soccer success. The kick taker has a dead ball and is under no pressure, and there is time for tall defenders to

move up from the back to put more pressure on the opposition.

For players, scoring from a set piece is a major psychological boost, the feeling of having outplanned and outwitted opponents topped off with the satisfaction of hours of training being rewarded. Furthermore, a successful free kick unnerves opponents, who will then be reluctant to give away another free kick. They might be less competitive in the next tackle, and again will be doubly anxious if a free kick is awarded.

Practise set pieces at walking pace without the ball at first, slowly building up to the complete movement against defenders. Teams should have a number of set pieces planned, each clearly identified by a given signal, probably a number. Keep them simple, with no more than three players directly involved. That said, every player should be aware of the plan so that if the objective is a back header at the near post, they will all be ready for a deflected or misdirected flick. Players not directly involved in the move should be positioned so that they stretch and distract the defence. Those involved directly should arrive late and inconspicuously. The less touches between the kick and shot, the better the chance of a goal.

Free Kicks

Direct or indirect, free kicks offer the best opportunities for set pieces. They also call for more adaptability than corners, because you cannot predict in advance the exact location where a kick will be given. It never does any harm to have two players lining up to take free kicks, as the defence will not know which is the decoy.

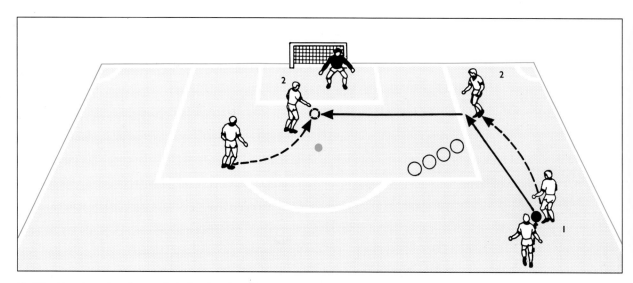

Fig 108 One player dummies over the ball, and continues his run to receive a pass from which he crosses behind the wall for a late-running attacker.

Beating the wall

A direct free kick awarded within shooting distance will invariably involve the defence setting up a wall to protect part of the goal, and the goalkeeper covering the rest. Obviously the direct shot is the best weapon if the defensive wall looks weak or is badly placed. Bending a shot round or over the wall calls for a specialist player, but is certainly a major threat to the opponents. Tapping the ball to one side to allow a shot past the wall is an excellent alternative. Have people available on both sides to keep options open and to allow a decoy run. If a wall is in place, it is taking up defensive resources, and the attacking team can afford to bring more players up.

Placing attackers in the wall unsights the

Fig 109 The ball is passed across, and the defence will follow it, fearing a shot. A chip over to where the kick taker has moved creates the opening.

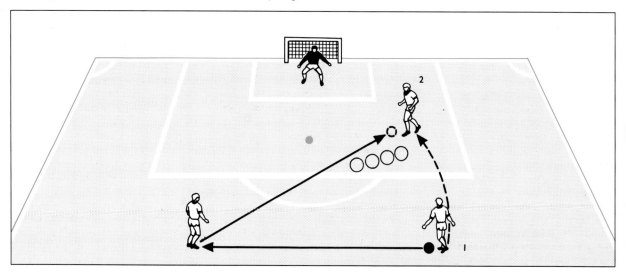

Fig 110   A player in front of the wall can deflect a pass either side, bypassing the wall and allowing a shot nearer the goal.

goalkeeper and causes confusion, especially if they break away at the last second. Putting a small, quick player in front of it helps too, as he can meet a short kick and turn it into someone's path, changing the angle of the shot and gaining a few extra yards. If two players line up to take a shot, defenders will expect the first to be on a dummy run. Yet he can play the ball to the player in front of the wall and move in for the lay off.

Crossing from free kicks

Again, decoy runs are a major weapon here, but the emphasis shifts from getting an angle for a shot to creating space in the defence. Early moves by attackers in the box can pull defenders across, leaving room for a late running full-back to meet the cross. A winger stationed to one side will be marked, but if he runs across the path of a potential cross or shot, he will take a defender with him.

Corners

The priority at corner kicks is to prevent the goalkeeper gathering the cross. So in theory long crosses should be floated or

swung round or away from the goalkeeper, and short crosses should be met and diverted above or past him. In fact it pays to be pragmatic and assess the goalkeeper's style of play. If he dominates his area and attacks the ball, curve the ball away from the goal to prevent his move, or better, to tempt him into straying well out from his goal for a ball that is getting further away from him by the second. If he is a bit jumpy, unnerve him by swinging corners in and putting him under pressure.

Defenders will be very familiar with the various corner ploys as they face them so often, so target men must start their runs very deep to have an element of surprise. Variation is important too. It is surprising how often even professionals fall into the rut of trying the same type of corner throughout a game. They may be aiming

for perfection in the move, but to the defenders countering, the threat becomes a routine. The hard, driven corner is an excellent option as a ball speeding into the danger area is always difficult to defend against and even half-touches can bring a goal opportunity.

In corner set pieces, as at crossed free kicks, the aim is to drag defenders away from the danger area, opening up gaps for late runners to exploit.

The short corner   Short corners entice defenders away from the penalty area, creating space behind them. The ball is tapped to a colleague and the taker runs back up the pitch to stay on side and collect a return pass if necessary. If opponents counteract this by bringing over a winger as a spare defender, the full-back will be free to take a deeper cross, and by drawing two players out of the box the possibilities from a deep cross are increased.

The near-post corner   A ball struck towards the near post and headed on at an angle is one of the most effective corner ploys as it is so hard to defend against because it has so many variations.

Fig 111   The short corner allows a long ball to be played into space created by attackers making decoy runs.

Do not rely on one player to flick the ball on. Rather use a short player nearest the ball supported 2yd (2m) behind by a tall player. The tall player will block the defenders' line of sight of the first man, and can attack a higher cross that the shorter man cannot reach. The cross should be struck firmly, not lofted, and should arrive towards the near post just above head-height. The near-post attackers may be content to wait in place for the ball, or to make runs from different angles to meet it. Once the team is familiar with more intricate moves, you could have a player positioned for a near-post cross who moves away, leaving space for two colleagues to attack the cross.

The long corner   Long corners, struck to the back half of the penalty area or the far post, are not as likely to produce a goal as a near-post corner because they are

Fig 112   The near-post corner headed at an angle is very difficult to defend against.

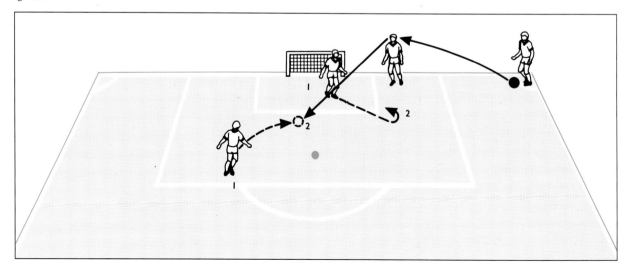

easier to defend against. The defence has more time to assess the threat, the goalkeeper can attack the ball, and the cross has to be accurate over a longer distance. However, as a variation, or as a ploy in which players make runs pulling defenders out, it can produce good results. Tall players should make late runs from the edge of the box, probably on a curve as this will disorientate defenders who tend to lose track of where the ball is as they concentrate on keeping close to their opponent.

Throw-Ins

The tactical aspect of throw-ins is a neglected area of the game. Throw-ins in the attacking third of the pitch are advantageous as a player can take his time and is under no pressure to pass the ball, on this occasion with his hands. That said, they are generally best taken quickly to maintain momentum in attack, and the golden rule is to throw the ball forward.

The simplest throw-in involves the receiver returning the ball to the unmarked thrower. The direct pass should be to head or chest, and should not bounce up at the receiver. As a pass, the

---

RULES CHECK

The thrower must face the field of play and have both feet on or behind the touch-line. The ball must be held in both hands which must deliver the ball from behind and over the head.

---

thrown ball should be put into space for a moving colleague who has resisted the temptation to get too close. Remember that you cannot be offside from a throw-in, so be prepared to treat the throw-in as a through-pass if the situation is right.

The Long Throw

Once you have a player on the team with a good, long throw, treat the throw as a near-post corner, and practise moves in which he picks out a late running target man to shoot or flick on the ball.

Attacking from the Back

Defenders arriving in the opposing penalty area pose problems as they are usually extra men who have not been tracked as they progressed up the field. We have already looked at the value of the overlapping full-back, but in more central positions it is imperative that defenders who move up the pitch are technically capable of more than a square ball or a ballooning shot. They must also be aware that the longer they stay in attack, the greater the risk of them being stranded if possession is lost.

Tall central defenders are obviously ideal players to use in set pieces, when there is time to get them up the pitch. Other opportunities usually spring from interceptions, when the opposition is caught still moving forward. This is when the adventurous defender can make his mark, but there must be a team system in

which a colleague covers his position as he roams upfield. Defenders rarely make good dribblers, so they should concentrate on their passing ability and the wall pass to progress up the pitch.

Exercise

Set up a match of six versus eight in which the larger team has no goalkeeper, but has three defenders who must play in their usual position. These are the only players on this side allowed to score goals. They will learn the value of interceptions, and the usefulness of the one two wall pass as they move upfield.

Counter-Attacking

All players would agree that attack begins the moment the ball is won. But fewer seem to believe that counter-attacking begins the moment the opposition wins the ball. By applying pressure, be it on the back four or a winger in full flight, players are making it harder for the opposition to advance, and more likely for them to give the ball away.

Once possession has been gained from a full-scale attack, speed is the crucial element in a rapid counter-attack. At least one forward should be positioned wide to receive and carry the ball, while supporting attackers make their runs to meet a cross. Just as important is the role of the rest of the team in supporting the move, pushing up to get the opposition out of the half, and ready to pick up loose balls from clearances.

CHAPTER 14

MIDFIELD

Midfield is the battleground of the modern game. Dominate here, and you ought to convert your superiority into goals. Yet this section of the book is shorter than the chapters on attack and defence tactics. Why? Because midfield is about attacking and defending. No one enjoys playing in, or watching a match in which the ball is rolled across the field for minutes at a time. So midfield players should read Chapters 13 and 15 and try to incorporate both sets of skills and ideas into their play.

Some pundits claim that the ideal midfield includes three types of player: one who acts as a deep attacker and pushes up to support the forward line; a central 'general' who is the link within the link of the midfield as a whole (a role usually suited to more experienced players); and the all-purpose ball-winning player. In fact, every player on the pitch should be a ball-winner whenever possible, and the creative/defensive midfield roles are best offered by two players who may have particular strengths, but who do not play in a set mode. While the 'general' patrols the central area, the other two players each cover one side of the pitch.

Midfielders need to be adaptable, and should be comfortable in any midfield role. Each should appear regularly in both penalty areas. It is worth adding that ultimately the defensive midfield player is of most value to his team, and when forming a midfield unit, the accent should be on defensive qualities from the unit as a whole. That said, any unbalanced practice game in which one team has more players than the other underlines the value of the extra man in scoring goals. It is the job of the midfield to provide the service and support to achieve this imbalance in a match.

Clearly, midfield players will benefit

from the defence and attack tactics sections in this book too. This is the price they pay for being the engines and the brains of the team!

Support Play

Midfield players have to be prepared to undertake a lot of unrewarded running in

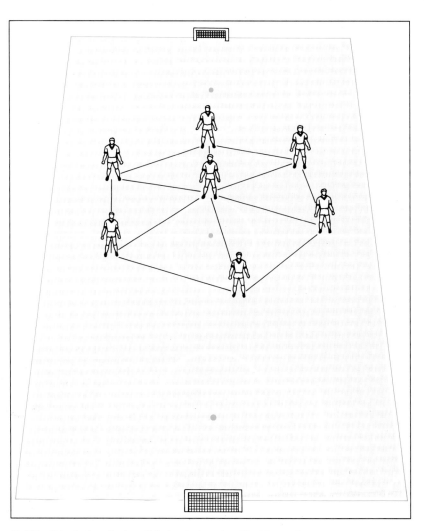

Fig 113   Triangles have the benefit that each player has at least two options close by of where to pass the ball. Much midfield play is based on the triangle approach.

Fig 114   Glenn Hoddle brought a new finesse to the art of the long pass from midfield during his England career.

the final two-thirds of the pitch, making space, giving players options and distracting defenders. They may not see the ball at all during some of the moves, but they still help to retain possession and to create opportunities for others. Clearly, stamina and an awareness of the patterns of play are vital here.

Exercises

1.   In a 12yd (11m) square have three players constantly on the move, interpassing the ball past one defender. This triangle pattern in which the man in possession always has two passing options close by is the foundation of much midfield possession play, and its influence can be seen at any professional match. Add a player to each side and expand the square to 20yd (18m), with the two players in the middle being changed if they win the ball or it goes out of play. It is important to

Fig 115   Supporting attacks are a crucial part of the midfield role. Here a midfielder arrives on a late run to outnumber a defence which is already coping with two attackers.

Figs 116 (a)–(c)   Support play.

Fig 116 (a)   An attacker skilled at holding the ball allows time for overlapping runs from midfield to meet his lay off. The ball is passed from midfield to the striker.

Fig 116 (b)   He flicks the ball into the path of the run.

Fig 116 (c)   It is met by the midfielder – in this case with a badly sliced shot.

keep space in front of you so that you have room and time to make your own pass.

The thing to remember with support play is that you are not supporting a colleague properly unless you are in a position to receive the ball. This is most likely to be at about forty-five degrees to the player, and away from an opponent. So midfielders must be prepared to drop back to offer better support, as well as to make runs forward into space or to take out a defender.

2.   Use the centre circle and ask two players to see how many passes they can exchange past a defender without leaving the circle. When they are moving well and creating space, use variations in which all play is two-touch, or add another player to each side.

Midfielders have to solve tactical problems throughout the match. If the opposing left-back is free to move forward, the midfield moves across to cover the area and puts a player on to the newcomer. If you are playing 4–3–3 against 4–4–2, you will be outnumbered in midfield unless you bring up one of your full-backs. So awareness and communication are important. On the technical side, balls from all angles have to be controlled in midfield, so first-touch skills need to be excellent.

Distribution

Midfielders make the judgement of moving forward fast or holding for a while, and passing ahead, square or behind. Obviously awareness is essential here. Passing will always allow faster movement than dribbling the ball, but dribbling does offer the benefits of building numerical advantage if you get past an opponent.

Exercises

1.   Set up a three versus three, and every minute or so blow a whistle to stop play and ask the player on the ball to shut his eyes. He must describe where his colleagues are and what he intends to do with the ball next. Then carry on the game.

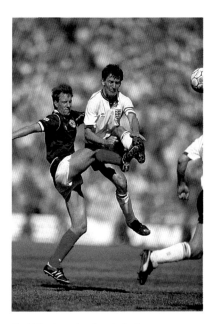

Fig 117 A rumbustious ball-winner with good distribution skills and superbly timed runs to support attackers, England's Bryan Robson is the model modern midfielder.

Build up the exercise to a six-a-side game, and ask the player in possession to state how many players are behind and ahead of him.

2. Ask one team in a practice game to play to one strategy, be it always to hit the ball to a target man, go down the wings, or whatever. The onus will fall on the midfield players to achieve this whatever position they find themselves in. This will be excellent unit-building work for them as they combine to meet the objective.

The Long Ball

Long passes struck from the midfield area are an efficient form of rapid attack. It is important to try to make the pass land behind a defender. Curving the ball with

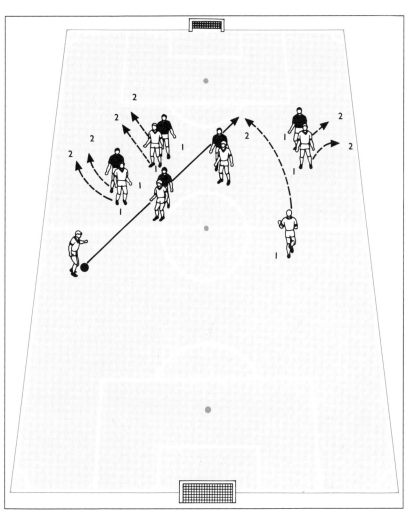

Fig 118 The long through-pass can cut out a congested midfield, but it requires skilful running as well as accuracy in striking the ball.

the inside or outside of the foot will help to get the ball round defenders and into the path of the attacker. If the opposition is playing a sweeper system, long passes will be forced in a direction more towards the wings.

Against a zonal defence (or a poor sweeper) long passes down the centre to meet angled runs by forwards should provide some opportunities, and this pass in particular meets the requirement of minimizing the number of passes made before attacks can then be created on the goal.

CHAPTER 15

DEFENCE

There is a difference in rationale between setting tactics for attack and for defence. Attack tactics are designed in part at least to raise players' awareness of the options that will be available, and to channel their efforts effectively. At the lower levels, a lot can be achieved with some gifted and enthusiastic players.

Defence tactics, on the other hand, are central to team play: they are the vehicle for organizing the whole defence, and only organized defences stop goals. Today's defenders need good tactical sense, because they have to adjust their play throughout a match to counter the various forms of attack. Because this kind of rethinking and repositioning can only be trained for in general terms (every match situation is different) defenders must

respond quickly and communicate well to keep the opposition frustrated. They must also master the basics of positioning: the rule is always to be between your opponent and the ball, to look for interceptions (the best way to restrict his use of the ball is never to let him get it in the first place), and to limit the space in which he can receive the ball without getting so close that you can be turned.

There are two systems of defence – man-for-man, and zonal marking.

The Zonal System

In the zonal system, the pitch is divided into four zones, each covered by one member of the back four. The zones act as

guide-line areas only and are never regarded as the limit beyond which players should not travel. In the British game, zonal marking is seen as the most efficient form of defence.

Split the pitch lengthwise into three with the central area being the widest. The full-backs cover one side each, while the two central defenders occupy two overlapping central zones.

As attackers move between zones they have to be 'handed over', so good communication is essential in this system. So, if the opposing right winger is carrying the ball down his touch-lines, he is marked by the left-back. If he cuts inside and moves across the pitch, he is handed over to the defender in the adjacent zone, and so on if necessary right across the pitch.

Fig 119   The zonal defence system, in which each player has an area to cover. Note the overlapping central zones for greater security.

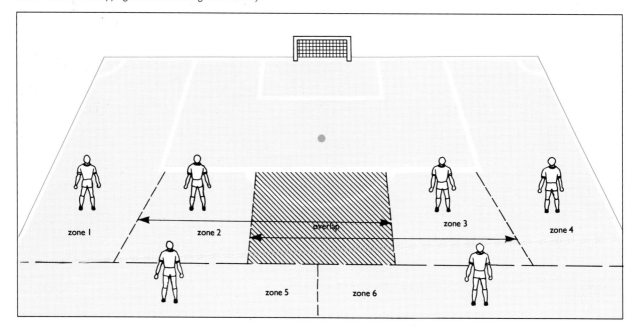

Exercises

1. Set up a playing area 30yd (27m) long and 15yd (14m) wide for a two-a-side game, to be played initially at jogging pace. The attackers will switch positions while the defenders must apply pressure, support each other, and prevent one-on-one situations. Now increase the size of the pitch and add a player to each side, and introduce the offside rule. The defender at the back represents the line to hold. Now move up to a full-sized pitch and use four defenders with two midfielders in front, and a target man on the half-way line to reach for clearances. They will face three attackers and two midfielders, whose brief is to switch positions and cross over as much as possible.

This exercise illustrates the fundamentals of zonal defence: covering territory, being flexible to support team-mates, and using the offside line as a back barrier.

2. Now string four defenders across the back, and have one player at a time dribbling the ball across the pitch, to be handed over by defenders as he moves into the next zone. When this is working well, give the dribbler a supporting player who cannot receive the ball but makes himself available. Now defenders must not only hand over the man in possession, but should prevent the attackers dominating any one zone.

This exercise shows the importance of handing over all attackers, whether or not they have the ball. Defenders must never view the four zones as a set of rigid divisions: the lines overlap and the boundaries are elastic. Some teams play a zonal system but add a sweeper behind (or more rarely, in front of) the back four to cover for through-passes and blind runs. This also gives the defences greater capacity to deal with overloads in one zone.

Man-for-Man Marking

This system involves players marking

Fig 120   Poor defence organization shows as six players face Diego Maradona. Who was marking his colleagues?

individuals instead of space. Each defender is briefed to mark one attacker, following him around the pitch when the opposition is attacking. It generally uses a sweeper who covers the area behind the defensive line to pick up stray passes and players. The system can be highly effective in frustrating gifted attackers by denying them the opportunity to win the ball. However, it is dependent on having defenders in the team who are capable of

STAR TIP

The position is the all-important part of heading. It's much more important than the actual jumping movement, because it's harder to play against a forward who is coming in to flick the ball in at the near post.

Paul Parker
Inside Football, 17, 1990.

Fig 121   The man-for-man system relies on close marking of individuals, and a sweeper is frequently brought in as safety cover.

marking one man effectively throughout the game. Attackers train hard at shaking off markers, and once one is free, the defence is threatened. When using the man-for-man system it is imperative that midfielders and strikers adopt the practice too, so that deep runners are picked up. The disadvantages of players being pulled out of position become benefits once possession is gained, as teams can attack unpredictably.

Many defences in fact use a blend of the two systems, in which zonal defence is supplemented by the one-on-one marking of a key attacker who is known to cause a lot of problems.

The Sweeper

Various teams have experimented with the sweeper system at various times. In the British game the system is often dropped for two reasons: lack of familiarity of the system by the back four; and the lack of players with the right blend of skills.

The sweeper covers the vulnerable

area behind the back four, looking to support colleagues facing the man in possession. These colleagues can then commit themselves to a tackle knowing that they are covered if it fails, and can pick up through-passes and late running attackers. So the sweeper directs the whole defence from the perfect position behind his back four, and is able to see opposition moves being built up.

KEY POINT: PITFALLS

The major drawback of using a sweeper is that it puts the team a man short in either midfield or attack. So it is generally seen as a highly defensive system, suitable for defending a narrow lead, or for two-leg matches away from home.

The sweeper also has a valuable attacking role, as once in possession he is generally unmarked and has a clear idea of where his colleagues are. West Germany's Franz Beckenbaur was a marvellous

attacking sweeper through the 1970s, able to spray the ball around or set off on long, surging runs knowing that the opposition would take some time to pick him up – and in doing so would release another player.

Some teams put a player in a kind of sweeper role in front of the back four. Here he cannot interfere with the offside line, and acts as the focus for distribution as well as having the freedom to attempt tackles just about any time as he is covered by the back four. Nobby Stiles carried out this role for England in the 1966 World Cup Final to great effect.

A sweeper needs a blend of skills in tactical awareness, tackling and intercepting, and distribution. He must dominate his defence and many sweepers are also captains of the team.

Full-Back Play

The role of the full-back has changed dramatically over the last decade in two ways. First, because there are rarely four attackers to mark, one full-back is free to

Figs 122 (a)–(c)   Full-back play.

Fig 122 (a)   Full-backs should cover behind their central defenders if there is a risk of a breakthrough. Here two attackers are trying to work an opening.

Fig 122 (b) and (c)   The arrival of a covering defender, however, lessens the threat.

Fig 122 (c).

move into the attack, or to cover space towards the centre of the pitch. Second, the pace necessary for the modern full-back to compete with wingers and fast midfielders becomes a valuable asset in attack, and many teams now have at least one full-back who is keen to overlap down the wing or play some other attacking role such as hitting free kicks and corners.

Still, full-backs are fundamentally markers and tacklers, most commonly facing wingers, and the first few minutes of the game should be spent assessing the opponent. Is he faster or slower than you? If he has better pace, be careful not to get too close and be beaten in a straight race for the ball. If he is slower, you can afford to pressurize him more, knowing that you will win a sprint for a loose ball. If he has a favourite foot, force him to use the other, and in general, wingers are best coaxed towards the centre of the pitch, from where they cannot make the incisive crosses they aim to put across from the sidelines.

If the full-back has no wide player to mark, his priority should be to support his colleagues inside, and keep an eye out for attackers making late or untracked runs. An opposing dribbler who gets past the central defenders should never have the goalkeeper as his next challenger: the full-back should be aware of the threat and be ready to block his run.

Central Defenders

Central defenders (there are usually two in a team, covering the large middle zone) are the mainstay of the defence. The space they cover is the area where attackers most want to be, and they usually mark the focal point of opposition attacks. More than any other member of the team (except perhaps the goalkeeper) their mistakes are most likely to give away a goal. The majority of goals are scored within a 15yd (14m) arc of the centre of the goal. Clearly defence here is a pressure job in which reliability is more important than subtlety.

The two centre-backs must build up a near telepathic understanding, knowing when to cover, and when their partner is likely to challenge for the ball and will need extra support. Some pairs reject the usual central left and right positioning, preferring to use one player diagonally behind the other. Generally the taller player who is stronger at heading the ball goes in front to challenge for crosses, his partner being there to foil faster movements along the ground.

Aerial dominance is a must for central defenders, with the priority on clearing the ball away from danger, which often means giving away a corner rather than lofting out a header which a supporting attacker might feed on. Because they are tall, such players are sometimes slow along the ground, but speed off the mark and of recovery should be built up too.

Set Pieces

Set pieces represent a major threat as they give the opposition the chance to bring up extra players and carry out a planned and rehearsed manoeuvre which the defence cannot predict and which, indeed, will contain moves (such as decoy runs, false calls and so on) to disguise what is intended. Set pieces truly are a test of the organization of the defence, but there are a number of basic rules that should be observed:

1.   Concentrate. It is well known that some players allow their concentration to lapse when the ball has gone dead – they become liabilities.
2.   Switch to man-for-man marking.
3.   Unsettle attackers by jostling, moving, and calling – they will find it harder to concentrate on their role if you provide lots of distractions.
4.   Cover every threat, including possible late running attackers.
5.   If a wall is to be built, use attackers, not defenders, and do not expect the goalkeeper to set it.
6.   Warn colleagues of new threats such as blind-side runs.
7.   Leave at least one player up front as a target for clearances.

Free Kicks

A free kick awarded in the final third of the pitch represents a potential threat on the goal, whether or not the kick is direct. The attacking team will take the kick as quickly as possible in order to maintain the momentum of the attack, so the defence must be aware of potential danger from the moment the kick is awarded. Herein lies one major practical reason not to bicker at the referee (apart from the rules of etiquette already covered): arguing

takes up time and distracts other players from their jobs.

Building a Wall

In part because of the possibility of a rapidly taken free kick, the goalkeeper should not be the player to decide whether and where a wall should be positioned. This job should be undertaken by a senior defender.

Walls are needed whenever a kick – direct or not – is awarded in a position from which a shot could be struck, or from where a threatening cross could be hit (this covers kicks awarded at acute angles to the goal).

Defenders in the wall are wasting their skills. They should be marking opposition attackers, leaving the blocking job to forward players. The tallest player should be on the outside (the goal-post side) of the wall, with his colleagues following in decreasing order of size. He should be

Fig 123   *The defensive wall for a free kick should have the tallest player at the post end, just outside the line from ball to post to discourage a swerved shot. Players should then stand in diminishing height order, arms unlinked.*

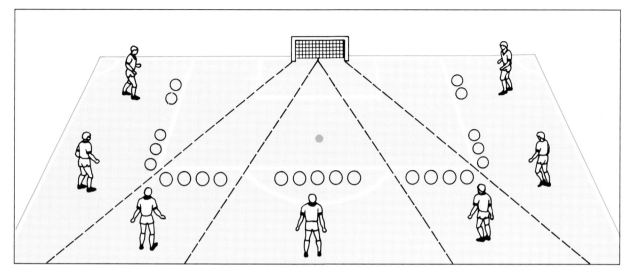

Fig 124   A rough guide to numbers typically placed in walls for free kicks from different angles.

outside the direct line between ball and post, to counteract the curved shot. He should take up his position first and keep his feet planted as the rest of the wall joins him. That way, there is no need to try to shift the whole wall along to correct any maladjustment. Defenders should be marking attackers or vulnerable space, keeping alert for the late runs and decoy moves which are part of every set piece.

The number in the wall is decided by the defender instructing them, but as a guide-line, five players should be used for a kick in a central position near the penalty box, while two players would suffice for a kick from an acute angle on the side of the box. The wall should be positioned to cover one side of the goal, while the goalkeeper retains a clear vision of the ball from the other side.

Players in the wall should not link arms (it restricts their movement) but should protect their vitals, and should be close enough to each other to prevent the ball getting through. This is not likely to be attempted: the properly organized wall acts as a disincentive to shoot, rather than a target around which to bend the ball. Opposition players should be prevented from getting into the wall, as they can seriously impair its efficiency.

RULES CHECK

Opposition players must retreat a minimum of 10yd (9m) from the ball when it is placed for a free kick, whether or not it is direct.

As soon as the kick is taken, players should attack the ball as a unit, maintaining the shape of the wall as much as possible.

Set pieces work for one simple reason: the opposition manages to create some space near goal, for a shot or a killing pass. The most common fault defence players have during set pieces is being dragged away from the goal, usually towards where the ball is initially played. An angled chip into space met by a late running, probably untracked attacker, does the rest.

Exercises

1.   Getting attackers to devise set pieces while defenders have to cope with the move as best they can is superb practice for both elements. Have different set pieces played from the same position to show the variety of permutations possible. Any that result in a goal should be

repeated until the defence can cope with the threat.

2.   Speed is crucial in building a wall. This can be difficult if attackers have a long way to get back. Choice of players for the wall should be flexible and the decision of the wall builder must be implemented quickly and without question.

Corner Kicks

Positioning

A player should be stationed at each post, standing about one arm's length from the post, and about 1yd (1m) into the pitch. This is partly to cover shots aimed at the corner of the goal, but mainly to give the goalkeeper more licence to attack the ball, knowing that his goal-line is covered. A

KEY POINT: PITFALLS

Goals most frequently result from corners at which an attacker comes in untracked, or where the defender fails to jump with him or fails to cover the knock-down.

Fig 125   Defenders' positions for the near-post corner. Note the player
10yd (9m) from the ball moves into the line of its flight.

Fig 126   Defenders' positions on the near-post side: two at angles in the six-
yard box, and another on the edge of the penalty area, moving into the line
of flight of the cross. The goalkeeper is positioned at the far post ready to
attack the ball if possible. Some teams would also have a defender on the line
inside the near post.

player should also be detailed to stand 10yd (9m) from the corner kicker to threaten the cross. He should stand just outside the anticipated line of flight, moving into it as the kick is made. From this position players are also able to attack short corners.

At least two players are needed to combat the near-post corner. One should stand 1yd (1m) outside the post, one just inside the corner of the six-yard box, and another (if available) in line with him but covering the front half of the goal.

For the far-post corner threat, players are needed just outside the six-yard box, one in line with the far post and one in line with the end of the box.

For all corners it is important to cover the area between the six-yard line and the penalty box, space where attackers will hope to pick up clearances and deflections.

The goalkeeper is the key man for defending corners, because he can catch the cross. He should be positioned just inside the far post (with a defender between him and the post), and as always should call clearly to indicate if he is going to move out for the ball. However, in particularly congested penalty areas, or if an inswinging corner is on the cards, the goalkeeper may prefer to stand half-way across his goal.

Marking must be man for man, with players standing between their opponent and the goal, but slightly in front to offer chances to attack the ball.

Exercise

Practise positioning for corners without attackers at first, giving defenders the chance to get used to how various kinds of cross are to be dealt with. When they are comfortable, bring in attackers but practise at least five of each type of corner before moving on.

Throw-Ins

At corners and free kicks, the defence is weakened by its inability to put close pressure on the man who starts the play. At throw-ins, the 10yd (9m) rule does not apply and a defender should be ready to

Fig 127 Far-post positions for a corner: the goalkeeper towards the back of his goal, off his line, and a defender an arm's length inside the post.

cover him as soon as he returns to the pitch, while team-mates move tight in on players who may receive the ball. At short throws the opposition will most likely aim to return the ball to the thrower on the line – exploit this predictability by threatening interceptions and forcing opponents to rethink.

Long throws should be treated very much like corners: mark the space behind and *in front* of players who might receive the ball, and cut off as much space as possible in the penalty area. Such throws are predictable on two counts. First, the preparation for the throw alerts the defence to what is coming. Second, the flight of long throws has to be fairly lofted, and therefore quite slow, and this then gives the defence time to react to the threat.

Fig 128   *Marking at throw-ins should be tight, with one player ready to move in on the taker, who often receives the return ball.*

Fig 129   *Italian sweeper Franco Baresi is alert, mobile and a passer of vision and accuracy.*

The Off-Side Trap

If there are less than two opponents between a player and the byline when the ball is played forward, and he is considered to be interfering with play, he is off-side. If he is level with them, he is on-side. Since one of these opponents is nearly always the goalkeeper, the defence clearly has the task of never allowing an attacker to be positioned behind all but one of the defenders.

Achieving this is tricky, and relies on good team play and communication. The defence moves out in one line at the moment the ball is about to be played. Attackers are then either caught off-side, or forced to retreat and to take the ball while travelling toward their own goal. The move should be co-ordinated from the

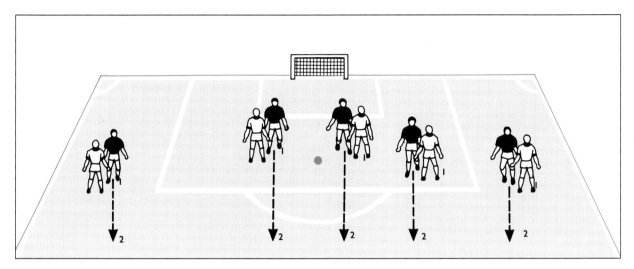

Fig 130   Setting the off-side trap requires co-ordinated running to a given
signal, whether it be a shout or raised arm, just before a telling pass is to
be struck.

centre by a player giving a signal (probably
a call) to move out, checking as he does so
that the line is moving properly. Attackers
will attempt to beat the trap either by
dribbling straight through – easier against a
defender committed to forward
movement in the line – or quick passing.
So awareness is important, but so is the
discipline of moving out when the signal
comes and trusting the judgement of your
colleague.

Because it is difficult to implement
perfectly every time, and that is exactly
what is called for, no sensible team relies
on the off-side trap as its main tactic. But it
can be effective in stopping attacks and
frustrating forwards, who will be slightly
more edgy the next time they are on the
attack.

Exercise

Get defenders to bunch into the penalty
area, interpassing the ball (not a habit to be
over-encouraged), before a central
defender clears the ball and co-ordinates a
move upfield. Once this is working well,
add two opposition strikers and a
midfielder. The midfield player holds the
ball and tries to make a through-pass

> **KEY POINT**
>
> Concentration is all in defensive work,
> and the time when it most often falters
> is just after your own side has scored.
> Excitement and relief occupy the mind –
> and you are more likely to make a
> mistake. In fact, 2–0 is said to be the
> most dangerous lead to have, because
> players begin to feel invulnerable.

(excellent practice for other skills here)
while the defence attempts the off-side
trap.

PART 4

FITNESS

CHAPTER 16

GETTING AND STAYING FIT

It goes without saying that good footballers need to be fit. They require a certain kind of fitness, though: soccer is all about bursts of speed which are repeated when required over the whole ninety minutes of a match. So stamina is as important as sprinting ability. Mental strength and ability is required too. Many top-class clubs contain at least one ageing player who is physically far slower than he was at the peak of his career, but has learned enough about the game to know how to use his resources, by making space, timing passes well, and getting into positions to support colleagues and threaten the opposition. Make a distinction between fitness training and skills training: you need both, and you can do both on your own or with your team-mates. Part 2 includes many training exercises, some of which will involve colleagues, but others which need nothing more than a wall or a few cones or pots.

Basic Fitness

Basic fitness is not something you achieve from training sessions: it should be part of your way of life. Avoid smoking, drugs, over-indulgence in alcohol, and ensure that you eat a balanced diet with plenty of fresh fruit and vegetables and not too much fat.

A series of stretching exercises first thing in the morning wakes you up physically and mentally. Try the following routine and expand it as you see fit:

1.   Stand upright with the feet slightly apart. Lean very slightly forward with your body forming a straight line. Take a few deep breaths.
2.   Keeping the back straight, slowly bend to touch the toes. Repeat 8 times.
3.   Place the legs further apart and lean to one side, bending the leg on that side so

that your head is being pushed over your knees. Repeat 8 times on each side.
4.   Throw one leg forward and bend the knee, leaning over it while the back leg is kept straight. Repeat 8 times.
5.   Place hands on hips and swivel the trunk round full circle, leaning over as far as you can without overbalancing. Repeat 8 times in each direction.
6.   Lie on the floor and 'cycle' in the air with your legs for 10 sets of 8 cycles.

These are simple exercises to stretch and warm up the muscles. It is a good idea to carry out a similar warming-up routine before every training session and every match. You may wish to add some stomach-stretching exercises too (see page 119).

Stamina

Every player needs stamina to ensure that he can make that final sprint as readily in the 90th minute as in the first. Jogging is an excellent way of keeping fit and of building up stamina. Try to jog a minimum of 2 miles (3km) at least 3 times each week. This should be built up to 8–10 mile (13–16km) runs. This advice does not apply to younger players, who possess plenty of natural energy and should devote their training time to improving their skills.

In soccer, speed and stamina must go hand in hand, so shuttle sprint runs are essential in any team training programme.

Shuttle Runs

Set up a line of cones with gaps between them at distances of 5, 10, 15 and 20yd (4.5, 9, 14 and 18m) from the starting line. Either individually or (better) in pairs, players must run to the first cone, return

to the line, sprint to the second, and so on. As a variation, tell players to stop half-way on each run, then start again. This kind of sprint exercise is far more useful than a series of 100yd (90m) dashes as it replicates the requirements made of players during a match.

Runs Around the Pitch

The soccer pitch itself is an excellent piece of training equipment. Get groups of players to jog the long side, sprint the short side, jog and sprint in a circuit. For a competitive training exercise, have two groups use the half-pitch as a circuit, starting at the same point on the side of the pitch. They sprint one side and jog three, then sprint two and jog two, and build up until the whole circuit is a sprint.

Fitness Exercises

The golden rule with all fitness exercises is to keep your movements gentle. Every gym has an enthusiast screaming 'No pain, no gain', but you must not force yourself into doing more exercises if the result is a series of uncontrolled, jerky movements. If you do, you could be heading for serious injury. That said, you must push yourself to improve your strength, and that will mean some pain as your body learns to accept a deeper stretch, or do an extra push-up. You must take a breather between sets of exercises too, to give your body a chance to recover a little and to set yourself up for the next task. Always ask for expert advice when trying something new. Another important point is that strength building exercises should not be competitive: the contrast is with yourself, not your team-mates. So keep a record of how many, say, squat-thrusts you can

Fig 131 Shuttle runs reproduce the demands of a match by forcing players into a series of short sprints.

perform in 1 minute and aim to improve on that figure in a week's time. You should aim to do a regular (preferably daily, but at least 3 times a week) 20 - minute exercise routine in addition to the team training sessions.

Fig 132 Dribbling between cones improves ball control and movement at speed.

Leg Strength

Examine professional footballers as they trot on to the pitch and you will notice that they share one physical characteristic, no matter what shape and size they are – strong, well developed legs.

Squat-thrusts

Lie face down on the floor with the legs together, hands at shoulder-width, and lift the upper body by pressing down the hands through the arms. Your trunk will be lifted up. Keeping your weight on your arms, and your hands flat on the floor, spring the legs forward to land under the body, then spring back to where you were before. Through the exercise you are squatting, thrusting the legs back, squatting . . . and so on. Time yourself once a week to see how many you can do in a minute. Then set yourself a target of twice that many squat-thrusts every day, performed in groups of 10. A week later, time yourself over a minute again to monitor any improvement. If you can perform 100 squat-thrusts in one go, you have reached quite a high level of leg strength, and can afford to concentrate on other areas.

Skipping (with or without a rope), and hopping are other excellent exercises for building leg strength. Try to do one exercise for 30 seconds, rest for a minute, then do another 30 seconds. Carry on this pattern until you can feel your legs getting heavy, and then take a break before switching to another exercise.

Upper Body Strength

While leg strength may seem to be of paramount importance for a soccer player, his stomach muscles are also vital. They build the upper body strength that helps to kick the body into action, and which is invaluable in shielding the ball and keeping an aggressive opponent legally at bay.

Press-ups

Lie face down with your elbows tucked in and the hands at shoulder-width, weight pushed on the balls of your feet. Now push down with the arms until they are straight, thus raising the trunk and keeping it in a straight line. Lower yourself again, in a controlled movement – not a collapse on to the floor. Repeat the movements until you find your body getting too heavy. Stop and rest.

Sit-ups

Lie face up with your hands behind your head. Pull yourself up into a sitting position without lifting your heels from the floor. (If you can't stop lifting your feet, wedge them under a piece of furniture.) Then lower yourself to the ground and repeat. A variation is to bend the legs so that the knees are raised, with the arms held out in front. Again, lift yourself up until your head faces your knees.

Weight Training

Weight training is not weight lifting, but a vehicle for building strength, not an end in

Fig 133 (Overleaf) Fit footballers have longer playing careers, like Gary Lineker who has been a formidable striker for many seasons.

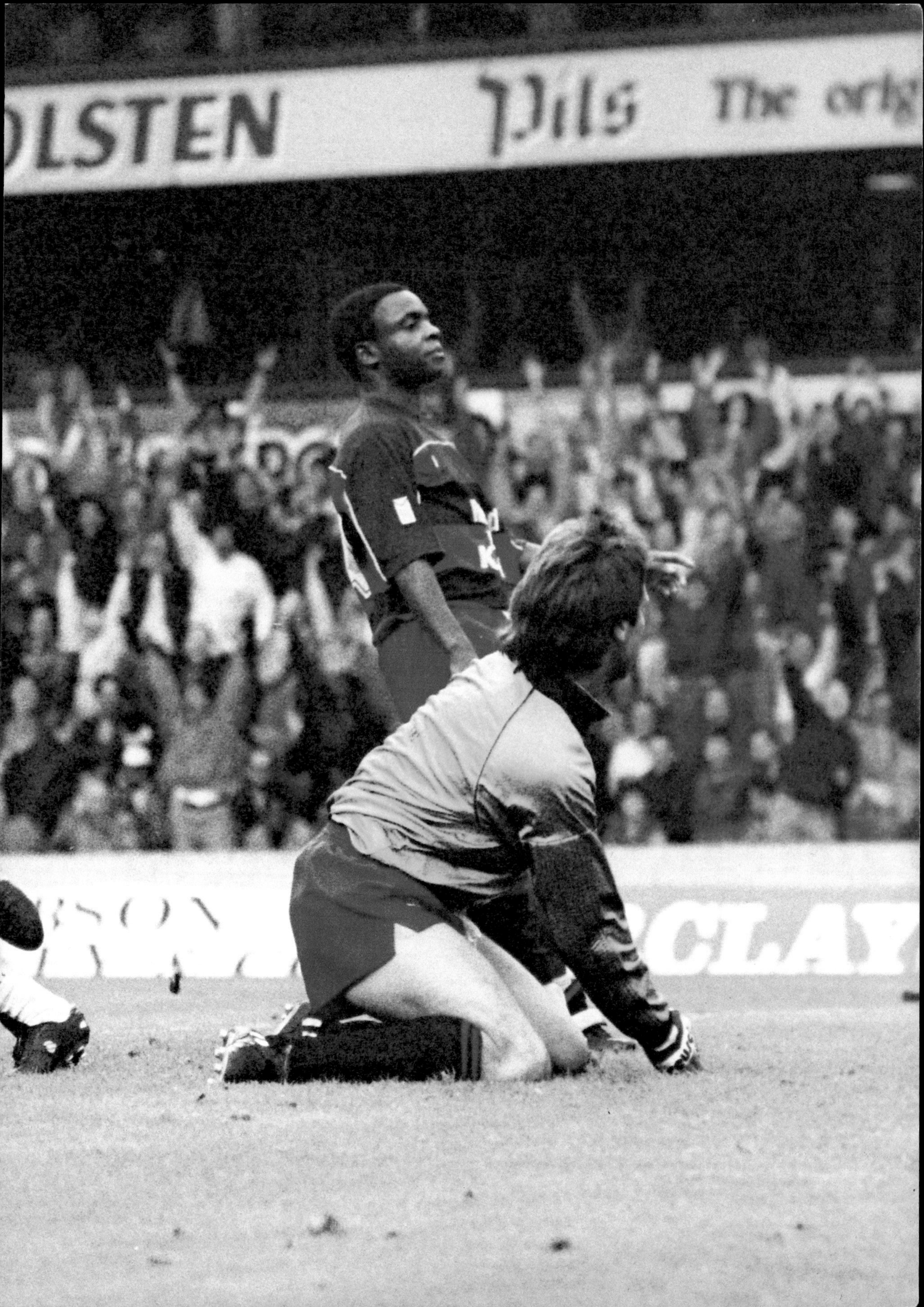
OLSTEN
Pils
The

Fig 134   Ruud Gullit of Holland is one of the most inventive and skilful players in the world – and one of his great strengths is his fitness and ability to maintain his game through 90 minutes.

carrying out some weight training is to fill two bags with sand and attach them with strong, thick cord. Experiment with the amount of sand until you have produced two weights which make the following exercises challenging but not a huge struggle.

1.   Lie face up on the floor with the weights draped across your ankles. Slowly lift your feet together to a height of 1ft (30cm), and hold for 10 seconds before lowering them slowly. Repeat 10 times.
2.   Stand with your arms down, elbows bent and hands by your shoulders, holding one bag in each hand. Push one arm up until it is straight, count to 10 and lower it, then raise the other. Repeat 10 times.

Training the Team

The team coach must plan his side's training programme so that it meets the fitness and skills improvement objectives, and keeps the players interested and motivated. Using a football as part of the exercise helps to maintain commitment, especially when there are goals to be scored. The best example of this is one-touch football, in which players can only pass or shoot with their one touch of the ball. It makes them think, and forces them to keep moving to help their colleagues by giving them a number of options of where to pass the ball. When devising training exercises, try to ensure there is an element of goal scoring in them: this gives the exercise a sense of purpose, and helps to keep the focus of the team's play on getting the ball in the net.

The Coaching Calendar

As conditions change through the football season, so the nature of each match changes, and the training programme should reflect this.

Early on, pitches are firm and fast – concentrate on ball skills, passing and team play. As winter nears the ground becomes heavier, takings its toll in slower, muddy pitches – so stamina training is more important. With the approach of spring,

itself. Using heavy weights will not build the kind of strength you need for soccer. In fact, it will slow you down. Always use weights under expert supervision, and use weight training sparingly, increasing the number of movement repetitions rather than the weights as you get fitter.

A simple and inexpensive way of

ball work should come top of the agenda again. That said, every week the coaching should include shooting, crossing, heading, attacking and defending as these are the mainstays of the game and no player can ever have enough training in them.

Mental Training

There are two sides to mental training: team bonding, and individual strength.

Team Bonding

Different things motivate different people, but a player who feels part of a team is more committed to helping his colleagues and winning the match than an outsider who does not feel an affinity with his team-mates. That does not mean that members in a soccer squad have to be best friends, but it does echo a truth from many walks of life: you try harder for people you share a bond with.

Just being members of the same team does not unite people. Bonding comes through building an understanding with each other, and mutual respect.

The coach can do a lot to foster this. Each training programme should include exercises in which players have to work together. An obvious example is piggy-back rides – good for building strength in carrier and balance in the rider, and highly competitive if you make it a race or a punishment! Or you can get players to run round the pitch as a unit, performing tasks such as sit-ups or skips on a given signal, again as a unit.

Forcing players in this case into close physical contact is a simple bonding exercise, but players should be involved in the mental side of the game, too. If team tactics are being changed, you don't have to involve them all in the discussion as to what should be done, but you must communicate the changes to them as a team and as a unit. That way, they all get to hear the same explanation, and can help each other understand any changes.

Some teams form two circles, one inside the other, in the changing rooms before a game. They walk round in opposite directions, greeting each other with a slap of hands or some bonding gesture. Other teams prefer a quieter way of showing their unity, perhaps by forming a circle and listening to one calm voice remind them of what they need to do. The choice of action will be different every time, but the principle is the same: form the team into a loyal, trusting unit, which knows that every player can rely on the others for support on the pitch. The psychological impact can be remarkable.

Individual Strength

Confidence is essential for a good footballer. If he has played well for a run of games, and feels mentally and physically fit, that should be no problem. But everybody has their off days, and no one can sustain 100 per cent confidence throughout their life. The coach can help here, and should because eleven confident, assertive players will perform better than a team that contains individuals who are worried about how they are performing.

Individual chats with players about their strengths can help – a bit of attention and personal tuition can work wonders. Visualization is another weapon in the armoury. Get the player (or players) into a relaxed frame of mind by getting them close their eyes, perhaps lie on the floor, and talk to them in a soft, but firm, tone of voice. Ask them to recall moments of excellence they have shown – in a match or in training – and to remember how they felt as they made that decisive tackle, tipped the ball round the post, headed in from a blind side run, or whatever it was. Tell them they can repeat moments like that, if they recreate that feeling of being in control, of being capable of doing something brilliantly without seeming to need to think about it. There is nothing 'spooky' or unnatural about this idea. It is geared to getting the most out of people, to helping them deliver their best. There is no reason not to follow it with a rousing team talk or a few words to individuals. People like something a bit different that makes them feel good about themselves. If it helps them enjoy soccer, why not give it a try?

CHAPTER 17

COMMON INJURIES

Soccer is a contact game, so injuries are inevitable at times. The first step to avoid injuries is to wear safety equipment such as shin guards. Shins are vulnerable and sensitive, so there is no point subjecting them to more stress than is necessary. A thorough warm-up before training as well as before matches will help avoid pulled muscles and strains. Many players also coat their legs with petroleum jelly to help keep the muscles warm during the game.

Bruises

Bruising is the most common soccer injury, and the most common mistake players make when they have a fresh bruise is to take a long soak in the bath. Instead, they should apply a crushed-ice-pack for at least 10 minutes. This helps to disperse the blood and stops internal bleeding, and if reapplied later it will help to restore the blood circulation. It thus eases pain and reduces the black and blue colouring of the affected skin area. Make sure to break the ice up into small pieces, and always wrap it in a towel, cloth or plastic bag: never apply ice direct to the flesh as this will damage the skin.

Cuts

Cuts and grazes are another common injury, and usually get filled with mud as the game continues. Cuts should be cleaned as soon as is practical in the shower to wash off the dirt (not in the bath). Bathe the affected area in warm water containing a disinfectant, and cover with disinfectant cream and if necessary a clean dressing. However, air is often the best cure for a cut, so if it can be left open it will heal faster. Cases of serious cuts (in other words deep cuts or those involving a lot of blood loss) should be taken to hospital. The player may need a tetanus jab or other treatment to avoid complications or infection.

Aches and Strains

A good soak in a hot bath can work wonders here, and massaging the sore area helps. Use both hands to gently pummel the area.

Cramp

The knotting of tired muscles that results in cramp can be painful and temporarily disabling. Sit on the floor and stretch the affected leg as much as possible, right down to the toes. Then massage the cramped muscles vigorously until you feel them relax. Roll up your socks to help keep a cramped calf warm.

Feet Injuries

Look after your feet: you can't play soccer with a foot injury! That means keeping them clean and dry. Cotton socks help here, and drying them well after a bath, perhaps putting talc between the toes, is good advice. Some footballers suffer from ingrowing toe-nails, which can be extremely painful. Get them treated by a chiropodist, and never chip away at the nails yourself.

GLOSSARY

Aerial combat   The contest for the ball in the air between two or more players.
Angling   Reducing the potential scoring area by moving to cover more space between the attacker and the goal.
Back four   The four players (usually two full-backs and two central defenders) who form the rear of the team formation.
Back-heel   Striking the ball with the rear of the boot.
Bicycle kick   Movement in which the ball is kicked with both legs flung over the player's head. A variation in which the ball is struck in mid-air while the legs cross over is called the scissors kick.
Blind side   Area outside your marker's range of vision.
Byline   The line linking the corner flags with the goal posts.
Centre-back   One of the (usually two) central defenders.
Closing down   Moving in on a player to restrict the amount of space he has to play in.
Covering   Helping out a colleague by positioning yourself a few yards behind him to enable him to challenge for the ball.
Crossbar   The horizontal bar which marks the top of the goal.
Cut out   To intercept a pass.
Dead ball   The ball during a break in play, including the period before it is struck for free kicks, and so on.
Decoy play   Making runs or moves designed to confuse the opposition and not necessarily to receive the ball.
Direct free kick   Free kick from which a goal can be scored straight from the kick.
Far post   The goal post furthest from the point of attack.
Flat-footed   A player caught unready for immediate movement in any direction.
Foul   An infringement of the rules in which a player has kicked, tripped or pushed an opponent.

Fig 135   Blind side.

Fig 136   Decoy play.

Full-back The defender (usually there are two) covering the wing.

Goal kick When the ball has crossed the byline having been struck last by an opposing attacker, it is returned into play via a kick from within the six-yard box (also known as the goal area).

Goal side The space between the goal and the ball.

Half-volley Striking a falling ball as it makes contact with the ground.

Fig 137 Half-volley.

Hand ball An offence in which the player is judged to have intentionally played the ball with his hand or arm. If committed inside the player's own penalty area, a penalty is awarded. The goalkeeper cannot handle the ball outside his penalty area.

Indirect free kick A free kick from which a goal cannot be scored with the first touch. Such kicks are usually awarded for obstruction within or outside the penalty area.

Inside foot The side of the foot between the heel and the toe along the inner ankle. Used for accurate kicks.

Instep Part of the foot in a line from the big toe up the boot to the ankle – the most commonly used kicking area.

Killing the ball Immediate ball control.

Libero A specialist, creative role in which a player is free to roam the pitch as he sees fit and to engage in attack and defence, although he is usually also a sweeper in front of and behind the back four.

Linesman One of two officials who patrol the touch-lines.

Lofted ball A pass lifted over a given space (usually occupied by the opposition defenders).

Man-for-man defence Defensive system in which each defender marks one individual from the opposition.

Marking Watching and tracking an opponent to prevent him from getting into, or benefitting from, a threatening position.

Midfield The area linking the attack and defence.

Nutmegging Beating an opponent by pushing the ball through the gap between his legs.

Off-side An infringement in which a player has less than two opponents between him and their goal and is interfering with play (in other words, could have an effect on it) at the moment a pass is struck (not necessarily to him). You can only be off-side in the opposition's half of the pitch, and being level with a player does not constitute being off-side.

One two Move in which the ball is returned with a one-touch pass. Also known as the wall pass.

Overlap A run outside, or less commonly inside, a colleague in possession, usually made by a defender supporting his attackers.

Penalty Direct free kick awarded in the penalty area for a foul or handling offence. Always taken from the penalty spot.

Penalty box The penalty area – the larger of the two rectangles around the goal.

Referee The senior match official and time-keeper.

Run-up The approach to the ball.

Six-yard box The small rectangle around the goal.

Striker Specialist front-line attacker.

Sweeper Defender positioned behind the back four, or more rarely just in front of it.

Target man An attacker used as a target for balls played from defence, usually briefed to hold the ball and wait for support, or lay it off to a colleague.

Touch-line Line running along the long side of the pitch. Also known as the side-line.

Through-ball Pass splitting the defence by going between two opponents.

Throw-in When the ball crosses the touch-line, play is restarted by a player from the team opposing that which last touched the ball. This is done via a throw-in from the place where the ball crossed the line.

Upright A goal post.

Volley Striking the ball before it touches the ground.

Wall pass Playing the ball to a colleague who returns it to you after or as you move past a defender.

Winger Attacker who covers the area along the touch-line.

Zonal defence Defensive system in which players cover space, as opposed to marking man-for-man.

Fig 138 The winger's position.

INDEX